A CUP OF C
10 OF THE TOP CRIMINAL DEFENSE ATTORNEYS IN THE UNITED STATES

VALUABLE INSIGHTS YOU SHOULD KNOW
IF YOU ARE ACCUSED OF A CRIME

Noah H. Pines, Esq.
Randy Van Ittersum

Rutherford Publishing House
PO Box 969
Ramseur, NC 27316
www.RutherfordPublishingHouse.com

Cover photo: khz/Bigstock.com

ISBN-10: 0692410120
ISBN-13: 978-0692410127

LEGAL DISCLAIMER

TABLE OF CONTENTS

ACKNOWLEDGEMENTS

We all want to thank our husbands and wives, fathers and mothers, and everybody who has played a role in shaping our lives and our attitudes.

To all the clients we've had the honor of working with, who shaped our understanding of the difficulty of this time for you and your families. It has been our privilege to serve each and every one of you.

INTRODUCTION

Contributing Author:
Randy Van Ittersum
*Host & Founder – Business
Leader Spotlight Show*

Our all-too-frail human flesh can often take over our otherwise law-abiding selves and land us in big trouble — with the people we love, with the people at work, or, if things go really wrong, with the law. When that happens, we can be propelled into a new and very sticky world of courts, life-long public arrest records, and permanent public scrutiny. It's easy to become entirely trapped — caught up in this web and it's notoriously difficult to come out unscathed. It's at these times when the help of a seasoned Criminal Defense attorney is essential.

Most of us have no idea how to choose an attorney of any sort, let alone one that has a long list of trials, like trophies, which prove beyond a doubt that he or she is a champion advocate. To find a lawyer with whom you trust your real estate transactions is one thing. To find an attorney who can save your life— literally—is quite another. When the lives of not just you but also your loved ones stand to be forever crushed by circumstances in which you find yourself, you need to call in the big guns. Between the covers of this book you will find the advice you need to locate the biggest guns—the very best in criminal defense wherever you happen to be — and to bring every advantage possible to bear on the legal problem you face.

DO I NEED A LAWYER?

Yes.

The first words most people utter when they find themselves in legal trouble go something like this: "I can't afford a lawyer." In *A Cup of Coffee with 10 of the Top Criminal Defense Attorneys in the United States*, you will discover the myriad reasons you cannot afford NOT to hire an attorney.

Put simply, the consequences of a conviction of any kind, but particularly a felony conviction, can and will change your life forever. Beyond the specter of prison time and other losses of liberty, including your right to cast a ballot or to own a gun, there are countless other penalties you must pay when you have been proven guilty of a crime. Even if this is the only black mark on your otherwise clean record, it will change the way in which employers, bankers, and even online love interests look at you. Why? Because your record is public and permanent. It's available for everybody to see. In this troubled economy, such a black mark can take you permanently out of the job market and prevent you from the pursuit of your version of happiness. A conviction can put you everlastingly on the outside looking in.

Like a life-saving surgery, a criminal defense attorney in your time of need can help you redeem the promise of a happy, fulfilled life. The benefits of recapturing this will far outweigh the costs. The insights contained within this book will help you to adjust your perspective, give you clues to the hidden costs of prosecution that could dog you for the rest of your life, and reveal to you the light at the end of this long, dark tunnel in which you find yourself.

WHY CAN'T I DEFEND MYSELF?

Even if you're a very clever person who has a clear vision of the way the law works, defending yourself in an honest-to-goodness court of law is equivalent to performing your own brain surgery. It's not just unwise, it's stupid. In most jurisdictions, judges won't even allow somebody charged with a felony to represent himself or herself. The consequences are simply too dire.

The legal system is far more than statutes and courtroom etiquette. Between the covers of this book, some of the best criminal defense attorneys in the country share with you the secrets of winning courtroom strategy: the things only an experienced lawyer who is familiar with the local system and the players in it can know, the things that can subtly nudge your case into the stack of cases won.

In this book, you will be introduced to the amazing skill set a seasoned, experienced defense lawyer brings into the courtroom.

Topics include:

- Investigating beyond the investigation
- Choosing whether or not you go to trial
- Preparing for trial
- Jury selection and how it can make or break a case
- Helping the prosecution's witness help YOU
- The importance of delivering powerful opening and closing statements

- What William Shakespeare and Clarence Darrow have in common

PROTECTING YOUR CONSTITUTIONAL RIGHTS

Of all the things this book can teach you, perhaps most important is the civics lesson that emerges from every chapter of this book.

The Constitution of the United States of America and its first ten amendments, known as the Bill of Rights, are specifically designed to protect the individual liberties of citizens. Within that great document are many protections that can be lost in the hours and weeks following an arrest unless you have an attorney at your side. Sadly, in the fog of crisis, many people give up these rights and more:

- The right to avoid illegal searches and seizures of your property
- The right to equal protection under the law
- The right to competent counsel
- The right to be considered innocent until proven guilty in a court of law
- The right to due process of law
- The right to remain silent
- The right against self-incrimination or being forced to testify against oneself (Does this include sobriety tests, you ask? Read on…)
- The right to a speedy, public trial
- The right to an impartial jury trial
- The right to confront your accuser and witnesses against you

- The right to call supporting witnesses
- The right to be free from cruel and unusual punishment
- The right to be free from excessive fines or excessive bail

The founding fathers knew that powerful entities like governments and law enforcement could become bullies if they were not carefully restrained. They had just fought a bloody war to free themselves from tyranny. Hence, the protections that are meant to give every single citizen a level playing field in a court of law in order to preserve liberty were created. Unfortunately, the adversarial system of justice we enjoy also has a flip side.

The other side is out to get you. The prosecution is not in the business of teaching history. Unless you actively demand your in-alienable rights, the other side is under no obligation to force those protections upon you. They will gleefully use your statements against you and happily search your home and car for evidence against you if you let them. Don't imagine that the Miranda warning will be enough to save you. That warning isn't always necessary, and anything you say before it's given is capable of being used against you. Unless you know and demand your rights or have an attorney that does, your life may change forever.

WHAT ABOUT A PLEA BARGAIN?

Every girl's father warns her about buying a car by herself. Dads know that there are sleazy car salesmen who will take advantage of his daughter's perceived inexperience. The lawyers in this book will each tell you about the perils of plea agreement negotiations, which are especially dangerous when the prosecution knows you have no advocate protecting you. We are certainly not saying that prosecutors are sleazy, but they are out to get a conviction with your name on it. If there is a rule as important to follow as "Never go to court without an attorney," it is this one: "Never undertake a plea bargain agreement without talking to a defense attorney first!"

Remember, the prosecutor wants to convict you. It's his job. Unless you know every last possible consequence of making a plea, you have no business signing away your rights.

REMEMBER JOHN ADAMS

If you ever find yourself asking how any self-respecting lawyer could defend someone accused of child molestation or vehicular homicide, this compilation can answer those questions as well. It comes down to this: "It is better for ten guilty men to go free than for one innocent man to suffer." In the world of justice, this bit of policy, also known as Blackstone's formulation, remains as an immutable principle of our nation.

The founding fathers of this great nation, who had only recently struggled out from under the fist of tyranny, made it a point to create the Bill of Rights in order to carefully corral and restrain the government's power when it came to revocation of the liberties of any human being. It is in the fabric of the Constitution itself that we begin to understand the need for our adversarial system of government. You will come to understand why the Framers insisted that there must always be Criminal Defense attorneys in our country to fight for the rights of anyone accused of criminal behavior.

A Cup of Coffee with 10 of the Top Criminal Defense Attorneys in the United States will open your eyes to the hidden world of justice: how it works, why it works, and, most importantly, how to make it work for you instead of against you. Consider this an investment in your future, because anybody can make a big mistake.

Randy Van Ittersum
Host & Founder – Business Leader Spotlight Show

1

A LITTLE HISTORY

by Noah H. Pines, Esq.

Noah H. Pines, Esq.
Ross & Pines, LLC
Atlanta, Georgia
www.rossandpines.com

Regarded as one of Atlanta's top criminal defense lawyers, Noah received his undergraduate degree from Emory University College in 1992, and his law degree (with distinction) from Emory University School of Law in 1995.

In July of 1995, Noah started his career by prosecuting misdemeanor cases in the DeKalb County Solicitor's Office. In 1998, Noah joined the DeKalb County District Attorney's Office where he prosecuted felony cases including: drug trafficking, rape, murder, armed robbery, child molestation and child homicide.

Since 2001, Noah has defended people throughout the State of Georgia in all types of criminal cases, including: juvenile delinquencies, misdemeanors, felonies, and criminal appeals. Noah's knowledge of the criminal justice system and the trial skills he gained as a prosecutor makes him an invaluable asset to the clients he represents. His meticulous trial preparation and knowledge of the law makes him a formidable opponent every time he steps into a courtroom.

A LITTLE HISTORY

I have been practicing law for 20 years, but I have not always been in private practice. I began my career in the DeKalb County Solicitor's Office, prosecuting misdemeanor cases. It was an invaluable experience.

The best place to begin your career as a trial lawyer is a place where you can soak up the most experience in the shortest amount of time. Working as a prosecutor in the Solicitor's Office is much like working in an emergency room or on the frontlines of a battle field because you are constantly learning under fire. You are in court almost every day, you are being bombarded by experience from every direction and you have to learn to think on your feet to survive. It really is trial by fire, but it's the best training you can get.

I worked in the Solicitor's Office for about three years before I moved to the District Attorney's Office to prosecute felony cases.

For the next 4½ years, I received valuable experience handling complex criminal cases. I started off prosecuting drug cases, armed robberies, and murder cases before I moved to the crimes against children unit. As a special prosecutor in the crimes against children unit I was in court almost every day prosecuting child molesters, child abusers, and baby killers. Prosecuting these kinds of cases allowed me to take the experience I gained at the Solicitor's Office to a whole new level.

After spending many years as a prosecutor, I was debating whether I wanted to remain a career prosecutor or make the switch to private practice. In 2001, my good friend and colleague, Peter Ross, called me and offered me a job. Peter spent years establishing a successful personal injury and criminal defense practice and needed someone with trial experience to help him expand. It seemed like the right time for a change and a good opportunity for me. I worked for him for couple of years before we formed our firm, Ross & Pines, LLC.

At Ross & Pines, I run the criminal part of our firm; I handle criminal defense matters in the Atlanta metro area and throughout the State of Georgia. I have literally handled thousands of cases and have tried well over 150 jury trials. Many of my cases involve allegations that are messier than most lawyers want to handle; I enjoy taking on these challenging cases. In addition to my trial practice, I have an active appellate practice in which I challenge convictions in cases that were handled by other lawyers. A big part of my appellate practice is finding mistakes that these less experienced lawyers made. I have written about 70 appeals and have argued before both the Georgia Court of Appeals and Georgia Supreme Court on several occasions. Knowing how trial issues are handled on appeal makes me both a better trial lawyer and a better appellate lawyer. My point is, I have had lots of experience. There is a reason why my cases have ended up on television and in the newspaper, and why I have received some humbling recognition from my peers. I hope to be able share some good advice here.

Going from one side of the courtroom to the other is eye opening. When I became a criminal defense lawyer, I quickly learned that not every prosecutor is as fair as I was when I was a prosecutor. As a prosecutor, I was interested most in seeking justice and making sure the criminal justice system was fair. Today, many prosecutors ignore these ethical duties and have a win-at-all-cost mentality. My job as a criminal defense attorney is not only to protect my clients' Constitutional Rights, but also to ensure that he or she is treated fairly.

Being charged with a crime is a serious matter. As a prosecutor, I would not just read the file and rubber stamp the officer's decision to arrest and charge someone. Instead, I would take the time to thoroughly review all of the evidence before making any charging decisions. For example, if there was a video in a DUI case, I would watch the entire video before deciding whether to file DUI charges. I can promise you there is not a prosecutor in the State of Georgia who does that on a regular basis. Instead, their decision to file formal charges is made simply by reading the officer's report. They will look at the video later, when the case is set for trial. It is crazy to me that a prosecutor would not take the time to review all of the evidence in a case before making a charging decision, but it happens every day.

When I was a prosecutor, my colleagues treated me with respect because I took my ethical duties seriously and I was fair. Now, as a criminal defense lawyer, I am still treated with respect by my colleagues because they know I am well prepared for my cases and that I am willing to go the extra mile for my clients. I am known for my trial preparation and my courtroom skills. Prosecutors know that long before the case goes to court, I will interview every witness, question everything the police officers say, and conduct my own thorough investigation. In many cases, I bring things to the prosecutors' attention that they did not know or realize. I know the case and the law better than anyone else in the courtroom. I outwork the other side; I have more grit than they do. I do not leave a single stone unturned and I never give up my fight for my clients' freedom. That is the kind of lawyer I am.

WHEN SHOULD YOU CONSULT A CRIMINAL DEFENSE LAWYER?

From the second you are suspected or accused of committing a crime, you need a good criminal defense attorney by your side. I cannot tell you how many times people come to see me after they talked to the police and gave a statement that is extremely detrimental to their case and their liberty. They come to me a year after they have been arrested and say, "I have court tomorrow. What can you do for me?" Instead, they should have come to me the moment the police intruded into their lives. It is amazing how many people talk to the police without first talking to a lawyer. Unfortunately, I cannot stop you from talking to the police unless you call me as soon as the police contact you.

Of course, lots of folks don't know that police officers are allowed to lie and they do it all the time to trick you into incriminating yourself. I have watched interview after interview where police officers lie and say things like "We have you on videotape" or "We have your DNA" or "Just tell us what happened and it will be okay." For example, I was recently watching an interrogation in a murder case. The police were interviewing a suspect who denied that he was involved in the shooting. The police said, "Look, we know it was self-defense. Just say it was self-defense and it is going to be okay." The suspect continued to deny being involved in the shooting. However, after more questioning by the police, he said, "Yeah, you're right. It was self-defense. I pulled out my gun and shot him because he pulled out his gun on me first." That man talked himself right into a murder charge because he is a convicted felon. Therefore, he is not allowed to have a gun and he could not use self-defense under the circumstances.

When a police officer calls you and says, "I want to ask you some questions" or "I just want your side of the story," your first response should be "Let me get your name and number and I'll call you back." Instead of calling the officer back, call a criminal defense lawyer for legal advice.

You cannot go to a doctor and say, "Doctor, I have this huge lump, can I have a free consultation?" But, you can come to me for a free consultation. The reason I offer free consultations is that I really, truly want to encourage people to seek out lawyers for help. There are many times when I tell people, "You don't need a lawyer. Here's your game plan." However, all too often people DO need an attorney and fail to hire one. Ultimately, they pay a terrible price for that failure.

If you take the time to consult with an attorney, you won't be blind-sided by the criminal justice system because you will know your rights. If you have been arrested, do not wait until your court date to get a lawyer. People wrongly believe, "Somebody's going to see my side. Somebody's just going to dismiss the case because they're going to see I was falsely accused." In reality, you have been arrested and the officer has written a report. The officer has already decided that you committed the crime and his police report is going to reflect that opinion. If you don't hire a lawyer as soon as you are arrested, then nobody is advocating for you; nobody is telling your side of the story.

The benefits of hiring an attorney are more important to your future than you may realize. I receive calls every day from people who were arrested when they were younger. They thought their matter was over. However, the internet has made it possible for their past mistakes to continue to haunt them. Now, more than ever before, you can be forever stigmatized and end up with a scarlet letter for being convicted, or even accused, of committing a crime. Unfortunately, some people think, "I don't have the money for a lawyer, so I'm just going to plead guilty." Then they find out they cannot get a job. Hiring an attorney may prevent you from having a record in the first place because the charges may be dismissed early on in the process. About 30% of the cases I handle are dismissed before the case even gets to court. Trust me, the money you spend hiring a lawyer will save you hundreds of thousands of dollars over your lifetime, making it a wise investment.

CHOOSING THE RIGHT ATTORNEY

It is the internet age, so most everyone looks for a lawyer online. That is a good starting point. Like any other business, lawyers market their services online. In fact, there are lawyers who spend hundreds of thousands of dollars on internet advertising trying to get you to hire them. This typically means that they have a high-volume business and they are probably not providing their clients with true, dedicated, personalized legal service.

Do some internet research—that is fine. But, understand that this is not all of the research you should do when looking for the right attorney. I always say, "If you know a lawyer, ask that lawyer for a referral." People ask me, "Do you know someone who does divorce? Do you know someone who does bankruptcy? Do you know someone who does business litigation?" I know the best lawyers in almost every field of law in Georgia and if I don't know the right lawyer to help, I know someone who does. You can also ask a friend, but your friend might want to know why you need a lawyer and you might not want to share that information.

If you have done your research and you have a few people in mind, look at their ratings on Martindale Hubbell's directory. Martindale uses top-rated lawyers and judges to rate other attorneys. You should also check the State Bar's website to make sure the attorney you are speaking with does not have any prior disciplinary history on file.

Once you have a couple of attorneys in mind, meet them face-to-face. I encourage everybody to come into my office for a free consultation. If a lawyer is not willing to meet with you for free, you want to pick another lawyer. If a lawyer promises you a certain outcome during your initial meeting, you need to run away from that lawyer. In my opinion, it is unethical to promise a guaranteed result in a criminal case. Any lawyer who promises you a particular outcome is lying to you to get your money. You are dealing with people, opinions, judgment calls, decisions, and juries. Nobody can promise or guarantee an outcome with these variables.

When people meet with me, they usually start by asking how much it's going to cost. To me, price should be the last thing we discuss. I want to know about you and your case. When I meet with a client, I always begin the same way. I get your background. Then, I want to know what happened and why you are being accused of a crime. After I've asked all my questions,

I explain the process of court and how the criminal justice system works. Then, it is your turn for questions. I know that when I'm at a doctor's office I don't want to feel rushed; I want to feel like I have had the opportunity to ask all of my questions. I was recently at the doctor's office with my daughter. The doctor was in the room with us for 65 seconds, barely introduced himself and did not ask me if I had any questions. It annoyed me. That is why one question I ask a lot is whether "you have any questions?" Make sure you ask all of your questions when discussing your case with an attorney.

THEY CALL IT THE "PRACTICE" OF LAW ON PURPOSE

To me, the most important thing in hiring a lawyer is to make sure that the lawyer you hire has the experience necessary to handle your case. I cannot tell you the number of times I have picked up cases from other, less experienced lawyers to find they have done nothing on the case at all. For example, I was hired on an armed robbery case in which my client was facing life in prison. The previous attorney did not do any investigation and did not file any motions. After looking at the case, I filed a motion to suppress the eyewitness identification of my client because I realized that there was an issue with the identification procedures used by the police. Boy, was I right! Not only was there an issue with the "show-up" procedure used by the police, but it also came out during the motion hearing that the eyewitness never even identified my client; the officers had lied about that. My client went from looking at a life sentence to a dismissal of the armed robbery charge he was facing because of the work that I did on his case.

They call it the "practice" of law for a reason. An attorney must continually sharpen his skills and learn new things. As a client, you should be confident in the person you are hiring, and confident that he has the experience to handle your case.

TRYING TO NEGOTIATE AN OFFER YOURSELF

Meeting with a prosecutor without a lawyer is a mistake. Prosecutors are trained lawyers and they are not on your side. In fact, the prosecutor's sole job is to make sure you are found guilty and are punished. Are there times when a prosecutor would make a fair offer? Maybe. However, you must ask yourself if he is telling you everything. Are there any problems with the case that you don't know about? Is there a reason why they are making you an offer that you don't know about? What if the prosecutor gives you an offer but you find out later that the victim or witness was not available or that evidence was lost? You just do not know these things unless you have the right experience—unless you know the right questions to ask. If I put the best divorce attorney in court for a criminal case, he would have no idea what he was doing. So why would you consider representing yourself?

PUBLIC DEFENDER VERSUS A PRIVATE CRIMINAL DEFENSE ATTORNEY

Some jurisdictions have very qualified, experienced public defenders. That being said, public defenders are overworked and do not have sufficient resources to devote to your case. They are in court with hundreds and hundreds of cases. Sometimes they meet their clients for the first time in court and plead them guilty at that first court appearance. Public defenders simply cannot offer the same level of representation that a private lawyer can offer. I deeply respect the people out there who are public defenders, but the system is broken. The system cannot provide a sufficient number of experienced public defenders to adequately represent people.

How Can I Defend A Guilty Person?

I represent two kinds of people. I represent innocent people who want vindication and guilty people who want mitigation. Sometimes I am literally fighting for my client's life for a crime he did not commit and sometimes I am just making sure that my client's punishment is fair.

Representing an innocent person accused of committing a crime needs no explanation. But how do I explain representing someone who is guilty of committing a crime? Let me explain it to you the way I explained it to my daughter's elementary school last year during career day. I started by asking her classmates if any of them had a brother or sister; most raised their hands. Then I asked, if any of them ever had a fight with a brother and sister; again, most raised their hands. I then said, "Let's say that your brother is annoying you so you punch your brother. You should get punished, right?" They all agreed. "Well, what if I said your punishment is that you are grounded for a year? Does that punishment seem fair?" They all agreed that punishment was not fair. Part of what I do as an attorney is to make sure that the punishment fits the crime, and that it is fair.

Plea Bargain Or Trial

One of my favorite judges, now retired, would tell every defendant, "Lawyers don't tell you whether to plead guilty or go to trial. They tell you about your options and the consequences of the decisions you make. Ultimately, you're the one who decides whether to enter a guilty plea or go to trial."

My job is to get my clients the best possible plea offer and then let them decide whether they want to enter a guilty plea or have a jury trial. In my experience, the only way to get a good plea offer is to conduct a thorough investigation and for the prosecutor to know that you are prepared to fight the case all the way to the end. This is why I prepare every case as if it is going to trial.

Some clients come into my office and say, "I just want to plead guilty." I tell them, "Great, but I'm still going to prepare your case as if it is going to be a trial." Some clients come into my office and tell me that they will never enter a guilty plea and they want a trial. I tell them, "Great, but I still have a Constitutional duty to discuss any plea bargains being offered." That is why I sit down with my clients and say, "Here is the offer. These are your options. These are the consequences of the decisions you make."

The work I put into preparing and fighting cases clearly pays off for my clients. I have a client right now looking at the difference between a 10-year sentence on a reduced charge if he pleads guilty (which means he will probably serve about 22 months in jail) and a 40-year sentence (with no possibility of parole) if he is convicted after trial. Ultimately, it is the client's decision to make, but the only way he can make an informed decision is if I have done my job of investigating the case, preparing it for trial, and explaining all of the pros and cons of the choices he makes.

YOUR MIRANDA RIGHTS

When are police officers required to give Miranda rights? When you are under arrest, or a reasonable person would believe you are under arrest, and you are being questioned by law enforcement. This is considered "custodial questioning." Obviously, if you are in handcuffs, it is easy to assume you are under arrest. There are questionable instances, though, when you may not know for sure whether you are under arrest and being subjected to custodial questioning. For example, when you are stopped and pulled over on the side of the road. The officer says, "Hey, where are you going? Where are you coming from? How much did you have to drink? Do you have anything in the car I need to know about?" In Georgia, the courts have determined that such roadside questioning is *not* a "custodial interrogation" and therefore Miranda warnings are not required. What you need to know is that regardless of whether Miranda warnings are required, you are not required to answer police questioning and you are never required to incriminate yourself.

For example, the officer may ask, "Have been drinking tonight?" Before you consider answering that question, think about the two possible answers to that question and the consequences of those answers. If you say no and you have been drinking, the officer will say, "I know you are lying, I smell something on your breath." If you tell the officer that you "had two drinks" then you've just incriminated yourself. Under either scenario, the officer is telling you step out of your car and you are probably going to jail.

While you are not required to answer the officer's question, most people do because they are not aware of their rights and because they have been taught from an early age to "obey" police officers. You need to be confident in asserting your right to remain silent. You also need to be aware of common tricks that police officers use to get a statement from you. Anytime an officer says, "I just want to get your side of the story," or "can you help me clear up some questions," you should immediately stop talking and ask for a lawyer.

If the officer does, in fact, read you Miranda rights, then there is no question that you are in trouble and that you need a lawyer. In my opinion, there are no circumstances in which you should waive your Miranda rights and give a statement to the police without a lawyer. The police officer may try to pressure you to give up your rights by saying "this is your only opportunity to tell me your side of the story," but that is a lie. Do not fall for it. Insist on a lawyer. You can always give a statement later if your lawyer thinks it is a good idea.

Despite my warnings, people will continue to waive their rights and give statements to the police without a lawyer. Based on my experience, every single interrogation should be videotaped. I simply do not trust police officers to accurately document what someone says in a statement. Even written statements have issues. In many cases, the officer is the one who writes the statement and includes details that he wants included in the statement. Worse yet, I've had cases in which the officer pressured people into including or excluding certain information in a written statement. Video cameras will help to ensure we correctly memorialize statements and also make sure that police officers are not using lies, tricks, and/or unconstitutional tactics to gain incriminating statements.

If I could leave the reader with only two golden pieces of advice I would say: (1) *consult with and hire an experienced criminal defense lawyer* sooner rather than later; (2) *invoke* your right to *remain silent*. These are the two most important Constitutional Rights you have and you should never give them up.

(This content should be used for informational purposes only. It does not create an attorney-client relationship with any reader and should not be construed as legal advice. If you need legal advice, please contact an attorney in your community who can assess the specifics of your situation.)

2

RESTORING FAITH IN LAW ENFORCEMENT — THE MEMOREX MODEL

by Anthony J. Falangetti, Esq.

Anthony J. Falangetti, Esq.
Falangetti & Weimortz
Long Beach, California
www.westcoastdefense.com

Anthony J. Falangetti has his roots in Southern California where the San Pedro native lives and practices Criminal Law. He spent nearly 14 years as a Deputy District Attorney prosecuting thousands of criminal cases for the County of Los Angeles. With more than eight years in the Hardcore Gang Unit, he prosecuted more than 40 gang related homicides. For the last six years he has teamed up with a fellow prosecutor to form his elite criminal defense firm Falangetti & Weimortz.

His excellence in criminal law has been recognized by commendations from the U.S. Congress, California State Assembly and Senate, and the District Attorney. He has lectured on defending public officials, homicide, gang cases and Miranda rights. High caliber work, along with an intimate knowledge of the system and its players makes him one of the most successful Criminal Defense attorneys in the State.

RESTORING FAITH IN LAW ENFORCEMENT — THE MEMOREX MODEL

There's a lot of tension in the United States today, and it can be seen in the news right now regarding police officer brutality. The situation in Ferguson, Missouri, is a prime example. I work in L.A. County. Just a couple of months ago, the L.A. County Sheriff's Department was embroiled in a huge scandal because deputies working inside the L.A. County Jail were committing crimes. In trying to cover that up, they conspired to hide their activity from the federal agents that were investigating them. The public is caught up with these scandals that center around the deterioration of trust in our law enforcement officers. I was a prosecutor for 14 years and have been a defense lawyer for the past six years. I have worked on both sides of the counsel table. I have worked hand in hand with the police, and now in my work, I have necessarily gone against law enforcement in this process. I have heard plenty of these complaints and the questions about whether or not segments of the community trust the officers, and there is a great big divide.

Most citizens who trust in law enforcement deal with them the least. If there is a lack of trust in certain portions of our community, it tends to be in neighborhoods that have the most direct contact with law enforcement and high crime rates. I think that is true, and it's very troubling. What should we do to fix it? What can we do to restore the trust in law enforcement? Opening up a "dialogue" won't work. That is just lip service in press conferences and newspapers. What can really be done to help communities trust police officers again?

Simply put, trust only comes through guarantees in proper police conduct and unequivocally providing the truth, always. In today's world, I think the use of technology can be used to accomplish this goal. Technology can help restore the public's trust across the board with our law enforcement officers and make our judicial system operate much better. We could move more quickly toward finding the truth. If we want to restore the public trust in our law enforcement officers, all officers and detectives should have a video camera and an audio microphone on them for every single encounter they have with a civilian. It will remedy so many of these issues, and we will have immediate and decisive information as to what actually happened. False accusations can be squashed right away and the truth can be seen and heard as it happens in real time. We can limit our inquiries in the criminal justice system to those moments that were not videotaped, or where civilians testify against other civilians, and the job of the officer will become easier.

I am not a fan of the cameras on every corner, necessarily. However, many horrible crimes and terrorist events that have occurred were solved because there was some form of surveillance camera that recorded information and evidence that the average human being or bystanders did not notice or see. That is great in those cases, but it doesn't directly go to restoring the trust and credibility of law enforcement. My first objective is to have them on the officer's collar. It is not expensive anymore. It is lightweight and it does not interfere with their duties. We will know everything the officer does when he has contact with civilians. When he interviews a witness, we will know exactly what that witness says. There will be no lack of memory or issue as to whether or not he wrote the information down incorrectly; we will have a verbatim statement. If the officer is forced to physically intervene, we will have the best possible understanding of the situation because we will have a videotape. The technology is available and it is affordable when you think about the benefits in relation to the cost.

I can think of three separate areas where having a videotape will result in immense financial savings. One is in the police department itself. Millions of dollars and countless hours are spent each year by police departments investigating their own officers because of civilian complaints. Those investigations will shrink down to minutes. You had contact with this officer? What happened? They will be able to pull the video and you will have a decision. For instances when the officer has to fire his weapon or use force to subdue the suspect and the suspect is injured or dies, as in the Eric Garner case, even if the suspect does not file a complaint, it must be investigated. Most of these investigations will be streamlined by watching the incident on videotape with audio.

With regard to the court process, it will also save money and time if we have videotapes. As it is right now, when I request information from the prosecution, they hand me a stack of paper that takes far longer to prepare than a DVD. If I can receive videos on the first day that I have a case, I can settle that case. If my client is responsible for what happened, then I can negotiate a settlement to minimize damage. A case that takes three months will probably be completed in a week. With videotapes, we can have results that are more accurate instantly. We need to settle cases to keep the court system running. The question is, are we settling cases at the cost of having innocent people convicted of something they did not do because the prosecution's offer to settle is better than what the person might receive if we take the case to trial?

Lastly, our municipalities and cities will save hundreds of millions of dollars in lawsuits. They will also save millions if they put video cameras on every street corner. The city of Los Angeles has to budget over 50 million dollars each year to settle lawsuits. This amount can be radically reduced if the only time you have to defend a lawsuit is if there is a legitimate issue.

Many defendants have the rest of their lives at stake when they are charged with a crime. If convicted of a felony, their opportunities in life are going to radically change. Some of these defendants are looking at 25 years to life. We need to ensure that we have the most accurate information before we convict someone of a crime.

While working in the hardcore gang unit of the district attorney's office for eight years, I tried 25 gang homicides. It was common for a witness to appear in court and say, "I didn't see anything. I don't know anything." However, their statements to the police were completely different. If the prior statement to the cop is on tape, the jurors have the ability to better evaluate that person's prior statement and why that person is saying something different on the stand. At the end of the day, if a person is looking at 25 to life and we have everything recorded, it is going to ensure that evidence is more accurate and the outcome more just. We can be more confident in guilty verdicts. We can be more confident in plea agreements. We can be more certain that people who are being convicted and people who are entering pleas are, in fact, responsible for the crime.

Videotapes will give us more confidence in our judicial system, more confidence in the result, and more confidence that the people who are being sent to prison are being sent there justly. More importantly, this will go a long way toward answering the growing unrest and mistrust the public has for law enforcement in some parts of the country. The public will have more confidence in police officers, because if everything an officer is doing is videotaped, then we can watch and hear the truth. Moreover, knowing that he or she is being taped, the officer will act professionally. Plus, I think using videotapes will also make the officer's job easier.

As a criminal defense lawyer, so many clients and so many families who come into my office are unhappy with the police and they are surprised by officer conduct. I have even represented a number of police officers who found themselves on the other side of the criminal justice system. When another person wearing a badge suddenly confronts them, they are sometimes being treated like a criminal. Suddenly they see things differently. They say, "How do you treat somebody like that? How dare you treat me like that!" The officer is surprised by the lack of respect he is receiving as a human being now that he is the suspected criminal.

Most policies dealing with technology like this are handled on a department-by-department basis. The city of Rialto completed a study that revealed using videotapes radically reduces the use of force in their department and reduces the number of complaints against their department. Rialto's police chief admitted that videotaping officers results in work that is more professional and that it also reduces the cost to investigate incidents. If we really wanted to effect change in the state of California, the state legislature should pass a law requiring all jurisdictions to use this technology. Unfortunately, there will be problems in implementing a law like this.

One issue will be the cost of implementing the law. All city governments and police departments will want state grant money to implement the requirements of the law. The central problem with trying to implement this will be an unwillingness to go all in. When it is done, it will be done halfway and that will not be sufficient to restore trust. To restore trust, we have to be committed. For any law or policy to work, there must be three main legal requirements implemented by every department and every jurisdiction.

- The first requirement is that contact with a civilian by an officer or detective must be recorded, even if it is a phone interview. If it is not recorded, the evidence is not admissible by the prosecution.

- The second requirement is that recording devices cannot be tampered with, turned off, or manipulated by the officer.

- The third is that every recording on every case must be turned over to the defense on the initial date of arraignment.

For any law or policy to work, there must be guarantees and real consequences for violations. Toothless laws are useless. Unfortunately, I do not believe that law enforcement unions will agree with such a law. The response will be that this is going to jeopardize officer safety because the officer will be so worried about what they do on tape that they are not going to do what is necessary to protect the public. That response begs the question, "What do you think they're really doing when they are not on tape that you don't want them to do?" If these officers are professionals and they are well trained, they will do what is necessary to protect themselves, their partners, and the citizens. They will handle situations professionally and justly, especially if it is being filmed.

On the other hand, citizen groups will have something to say about being recorded against their will. Keep in mind there is a privacy question that comes into play when an officer walks up to you and you are being recorded. As a defense lawyer, I can tell you that anything you say in front of an officer is basically being recorded in his mind anyway. I do not want my client going to prison based on human recollection. So, on behalf of my client, who is being confronted by an officer, I would much rather have the encounter recorded. I am not saying the officers are necessarily lying, but their lack of memory is rarely to the benefit of the client. I want my client to get the benefit they deserve, which is the truth, so I want the encounter videotaped. I am not necessarily saying these officers are being malicious or dishonest, but they are not always accurate. The first goal of our justice system needs to be reaching the truth. There might be citizen groups out there that are against videotapes, but the fact of the matter is, when you are arrested and the officer's statements against you are inaccurate, you want that videotape.

It is easy to say, "I want my privacy." However, the fact of the matter is that when an officer approaches you and asks to talk to you, there is nothing private about that encounter. If you are a suspect, you do not want your future resting on that cop's memory. That is why I am such a proponent of videotapes.

For example, in California during a DUI stop, the first thing the CHP officer does is walk the driver off to the side to perform the field sobriety tests. The video mounted in the patrol car faces forward, so the person is then off camera. When the officer says, "Your client put his foot down," or, "Your client swayed side to side or had to raise his hands to keep his balance and he was unsteady," I do not get to see any of that, because the tests we performed out of the view of the camera. Instead of arguing that this officer is exaggerating, fudging, making accusations or that he is not telling the truth, it will be easier to let the videotape speak for itself.

THE NEXT BEST PROTECTION — A GOOD LAWYER

In a perfect world, we'd have video and audiotapes of everything. We don't live in a perfect world, though. So, until those technological tools are put to work and you, as a defendant, have those protections available to you, you will need a good defense lawyer to act as your advocate in legal situations.

I have been on both sides of the courtroom. This makes it possible for me to see the system very clearly. I was a prosecutor for 14 years and I have been a defense attorney for the past six years. Some people want to know how I can represent someone I know is guilty. The answer is simple: I do not know they are guilty. The client comes into my office and tells me he is innocent, but the police reports say he is guilty. When I left the DA's office, former colleagues asked, "How can you go to the dark side? How can you represent these people? How can you represent people who are guilty? How can you represent people who committed a crime like that?" My first response was, "How can you just presume that they're guilty? How do you know whether or not they did it? Were you there? Do you have a crystal ball?"

As I was entering year number 14 at the DA's office, I had already prosecuted cases all over Los Angeles County. I had been up against thousands of defense lawyers. I had tried 65 felony jury trials. I had handled thousands of felony cases and thousands of misdemeanor cases. I had done it all. When I entered the DA's office as a brand-new lawyer, all I wanted to do was try cases in front of jurors. I always loved the drama of a jury trial and I became a DA for that reason. I wanted to stand in front of 12 strangers and express to them passionately what I believed to be the truth. I wanted to be the best advocate and the most dynamic advocate I could be. After 14 years at the DA's office, I had accomplished everything on my "to do list," including trying murder cases.

One of the things prosecutors do when they have a minute and are just comparing notes is talk about if they or a family member got into trouble, whom would they hire? My current partner, Joseph Weimortz, Jr., who also worked in the DA's office, and I often did that together. We would ask, "Who have you been up against that's any good? Who is it that you really respect?"

Joe and I began to notice that the list of people we respected as defense lawyers was shrinking. Joe and I also discussed how many defense lawyers missed key pieces of evidence or issues in cases. We began to think that the job of a defense lawyer should be done according to a higher standard and that we could meet that higher standard. I felt I had accomplished all of my goals in the DA's office. I wasn't sure I wanted to do another 20 years in the office.

I decided it was time for me to take on a new challenge and to try to accomplish something different. It is one thing to say, "I got a guilty verdict." However, it is another thing to say, "What would I really be like as a lawyer if I had to defend that case?" That became a different challenge. If I am going to say, "I'm the best lawyer in town," then I must be able to go in on the other side of that table and prove it from that side. I also wanted to be an entrepreneur. I wanted to start a business because, as a privately retained defense lawyer, I am only going to be successful financially if clients come to me and hire me. I have to be successful in the courtroom day in and day out. Clients want to hire Joe and I because we have a proven record of getting the job done for our clients.

A good criminal defense lawyer is able to speak clearly and in a compelling way, without notes, to a judge, jury, client, or officer. It is the centerpiece of being an American orator. When I graduated law school, I wanted to be on my feet in court, partially because I did not want to be trapped in a law library in front of a computer writing memos, briefs, and written work. So much of the criminal law practice in California happens without anything in writing and it happens in the moment, so you must be good on your feet. You must be well prepared. If you are not well prepared and you can't think on your feet, you struggle. You are not as eloquent and you are less effective. Your client is dependent upon the fact that when you talk, you are going to get your point across. You must be a good public speaker to do our job because that is really, day in and day out, what we do. If you cannot stand up in front of a stranger or a group of strangers and be dynamic and compelling in a way people will understand, they will not believe in you.

Another important reason why I became a criminal defense lawyer can be found in the Constitution and the Bill of Rights. American liberty is defined in that document. What is the essence of American liberty? A criminal defense lawyer is the only profession that is mandated by the Constitution to protect our liberty. The Bill of Rights does not require the existence of any other profession. Our founding documents require criminal defense lawyers because we protect American liberty. The second president of the United States, John Adams, was one of our most famous criminal defense lawyers. One of the most famous cases of all time was the one in which he defended the English soldiers who fired on colonialists in the Boston Massacre. Adams got them acquitted. It was the hallmark of what became the American justice system; in this system, everyone is entitled to a fair trial. The person who protects that fairness, who maintains the right to confront and cross-examine witnesses, who searches for the truth to protect the accused is the criminal defense lawyer.

I am a criminal defense lawyer because I do not presume anyone to be guilty. That is not the American way. It is my job to protect American liberty each day. It begins with protecting the person who is accused by the government of a crime. That is the essence of what America is about, and has been since the day it was created. Listen, they don't call totalitarian regimes like North Korea "defense attorney states." They call them "police states." Dictators don't send out the defense attorneys to squash their subjects. The totalitarian tools of oppression are police and prosecutors. The government takes liberty. It doesn't protect it. The defense lawyer protects liberty. We protect America from the oppressive totalitarian tendencies of government. Our founding fathers knew that to be true.

I did not have a political change of heart when I left the DA's office. I did not leave the DA's office because my political mind was somehow different than it was when I was a DA. When I was a DA, I believed in the Constitution. I believed every defendant deserved a fair trial and they deserved to be treated with the respect and dignity of a human being. When I became a defense lawyer, I still had the same viewpoint and I still knew that every person in America needed me. Now, when I defend a client and protect his rights, I am protecting the rights of every other American. If the defense lawyer does not stand in the way of the prosecutors or the police to make sure that they follow the law, they can break the law and run over citizens without limits.

Too much power corrupts. Police officers are allowed to arrest people. They are allowed to seize their property and they carry guns. Prosecutors charge people with crimes and they have the sole power to dismiss charges and to negotiate plea bargains. How do we make sure all of that power is not corrupted? Who is there to check on them, to make sure they are following the law and adhering to the Constitution? It is the criminal defense lawyer. Each day criminal defense lawyers make sure that the American sense of liberty and our right to freely walk through the streets of our country is protected.

Public defenders are doing a very noble job and they are doing the best they can, but the defendant cannot pick which member of the public defender's office represents him. As with any job, organization, or group of people, there are the great ones, the good ones, the not-so-good ones, and the really poor ones. The same is true of private lawyers. The public defender's office is no different, so one of the difficult aspects about having a public defender is that you do not know whether you are going to get one of their best lawyers or if you are going to get the not-so-good lawyer. Another problem is that public defenders are under-funded and over-worked. The average public defender handles too many cases at one time. They do not have the investigative resources necessary to adequately defend each person. They do not have the support resources necessary to do their jobs to their best ability. They are not funded in the same way that the DA's office is funded. When a state government issues grant money to fight gang problems, they send a lot of money to the DA's office to combat gangs, but they do not send money to the public defender's office defending the people charged as a result of the grant to fight gang problems.

If a defendant has the means to hire a private lawyer, it is the most important decision he will ever make relating to his future. Many attorneys are great at promoting themselves but not great at defending their clients. When hiring an attorney, the first thing a person should do is get right down to brass tacks numbers. How many times has this attorney stood in front of a jury and closed? That number tells me the most about a lawyer. After that, I want to know how their clients come to them. Are they an Internet-ad-based law firm? Do all their clients come from the Internet, or are the majority of clients referred from other sources? What are those sources? If the majority of the attorney's cases come from marketing, then that is not a good sign. If the majority of cases come from referrals, then I want to know who referred the clients to the attorney. If police officers are sending their friends and acquaintances to a lawyer, then that is whom I want to go to. If other lawyers are referring cases to the lawyer, then that is probably a good sign that this is a great attorney. In my business, the lion's share of our referrals come from police officers, prosecutors, and other lawyers. These are people that have seen us in action. After nearly 20 years practicing criminal law, Joe and I have handled thousands of cases, and the difference is noticeable. Those folks from the other side of the table know the difference and that is why they send us cases.

CHOOSE CAREFULLY

When you are meeting with a lawyer, the lawyer should explain to you how your case is going to proceed in the system. At the consultation, the lawyer should be able to give you his ideas about the likely defenses he will use in your case. If he cannot give you a strategy and his tactics to get you the best possible result, then he is not prepared to handle your case. You need to keep looking. You must also be comfortable with a lawyer. You have to be able to talk to your lawyer. Your lawyer has to be willing to spend time with you to explain what is happening in your case and explain it in a way that you understand. If your lawyer does not want to talk to you, then he is not the right lawyer for you. You must have a good working relationship with your lawyer. Your life is on the line. The lawyer gets to go home every night whether he wins or loses a case. If you lose your case, you might go to jail or prison.

GOOD LAWYERS ARE NOT CHEAP. CHEAP LAWYERS ARE NOT GOOD

That is the bottom line. The fact of the matter is if a lawyer is cheap, it means he is not putting in the time. I value my time. When I charge someone money, it is because I have to expend my time and my effort on their behalf. I have the talent, skill, and experience to get terrific results for my clients, so I am going to charge accordingly. Attorneys that do not value their own time don't value their own capability and are not willing to put the time and effort into your case. I would say to a client, "If you're diagnosed with cancer, you wouldn't go find the cheap doctor. You would find the best oncologist and worry about the money later. So why is the risk of spending the rest of your life rotting in prison any different?"

PRESERVING YOUR RIGHTS AND LIBERTIES

As an attorney, I wish that I could talk to people before they are arrested to help them understand how to protect their rights. A vital protection in the Constitution of the United States that protects our liberty is the right to remain silent. This keeps us free from being forced to incriminate ourselves. It is one of our most important rights. Do not throw it away. If an officer wants to talk to you because you are a suspect in a crime, do not give up your right to remain silent. Exercise it. Invoke your right to remain silent and ask for a lawyer. Once you give up that right to be free from incriminating yourself, you cannot take those statements back. They *will* be used against you in a court of law.

In America, it's never the defendant's obligation to help the government prove that he is guilty. In fact, it is the opposite. It is the government's burden to prove your guilt beyond reasonable doubt. Never feel obligated to talk to the cops and give them what they want. It is their obligation to get it whether you speak or not. The second you give up your right to remain silent is the second you help them prove the case against you. When an officer wants to talk to you because you are a suspect in a crime, there is really only one reason. He might tell you he wants to talk to you because he is looking for your side of the story, but 99% of the time that is not what he wants. He wants you to prove the case against yourself for him because without your statement, he has no case. Most of the time, detectives desperately want to talk to a suspect because they need the suspect's statement to prove their guilt. Never give them the opportunity.

I always say, "Do not lie to the cops." Therefore, the question becomes, "Is honesty the best policy?" The best policy is, "Never lie and never talk." Never lie; it only gets you into trouble. Never talk; it only helps the prosecution. Unfortunately, officers provide you with versions—or stories, hoping that you adopt them as your statement. It's just a trap. They are trying to trick you. He is inviting you to lie because if he catches you in the lie, he will use that to say that you are guilty. Worse yet, the truth may have been exonerating. Let the lawyers decide whether the truth helps or hurts.

The harsh reality is that the laws in our state allow detectives or police officers to look straight at a suspect and lie to them in an effort to entice them to make statements that are incriminating. One way this is done is officers will say, "We have your fingerprints," or, "We have your DNA." Most of the time, those claims are completely fabricated.

Obviously, when cops write their report, they do not write, "I lied to the suspect and told him I had his DNA," or, "I lied to the suspect and told him he was identified." He says, "I used a ruse by saying X, Y, Z, and in response to that, the suspect began talking and he told me that he was involved in the crime."

I will never forget one of the police officers I had as a client. He talked to the police because he said, "I have nothing to hide." He proceeded to provide them with corroborating evidence against him, which led to him being charged with the crime. He finally understood why the right to remain silent was so important. I said, "Did you say anything in your statement to that officer that, in your mind, equaled that you were guilty?" He said, "No. Everything I told him was the truth, and everything I told him showed I was innocent."

I said, "Really? You corroborated everything in the case except for the crime. They took your statement to prove that you were present at the time of the events, you had control over the person who was allegedly injured, and you committed certain acts." He made their case for them. I said, "Without you, they'd have had no case. They wouldn't have charged you if you had zipped it up and remained silent. Instead, you made your statement. As much as you think it exonerated you, they used different pieces of it to corroborate the accusations, which then led to you being charged." This happens to people all the time. It is one of the reasons why the right to remain silent exists, and it is one of the reasons why it is so important. Many people in our society have lost sight of why these rights are valuable to American liberty and why they are cornerstones to our justice system.

Another issue I see in our criminal justice system is the idea that putting a victim on trial is somehow wrong. I hate the expression, "How can you put the victim on trial?" The Constitution guarantees each of us the right to confront and cross-examine the witnesses against us. It is a fundamental element of our judicial system. If the victim is accusing my client of something wrong and I do not attack that person's credibility, if I do not question that person in front of the jury, how is my client being defended? The essence of the American justice system is the right to confront and cross-examine the witnesses against you.

Why should we let the accuser say whatever he wants to say and never once challenge him? Is that justice? Of course, it is not. Am I not entitled to present a defense to show that the accuser was, in fact, the initial aggressor? How does one ever present the right to self-defense without putting the victim on trial? That is inherently the right of self-defense. My client did not strike first because it was the "victim" who assaulted my client first. If you can't put the victim on trial, you have no right to present a defense in court, no right to cross examine, and no right to defend yourself against violence. That is simply not consistent with the Bill of Rights, and it sure as hell isn't what I would call American justice. Therefore, the expression "How could you put the victim on trial?" is ignorant of and inconsistent with the very principles of the American justice system. It is meant to be inflammatory, emotional, and built around the presumption of guilt. Of course, let's not forget, it is designed to demonize the defense lawyer.

Another cliché that I hate is "the defendant got off on a technicality." This is such a moronic statement. When police officers violate your rights, it's not a technicality. Nor is it okay because he wears a badge. Violating the Constitution is breaking the law. When a defendant is convicted, we don't say they're guilty of a technicality. No, they're guilty of breaking the law. So why is it any different when the police break the law? That is a technicality? In my humble opinion, the United States Constitution is not a technicality. It's law. And more than 200 years of American liberty should not be dismissed by some shallow cliché from a "B"-grade movie script.

Most people who fall into this trap truly believe that they want other people in our society to be moral. They believe that murder is a horrible injustice and it is a crime for which people should be held accountable under the law. They want criminals to be punished because crime hurts all of us. And that's true. I want our communities to safe as much as anyone. I want our officers on the street stopping crime and apprehending those people responsible. But I want it done the right way: justly, honestly, and legally. Many of us forget that we have so much more to lose if we sacrifice the principles of American liberty for the sake of convictions. We forget because we have it so good in this country. The greatest flaw in American exceptionalism is that we take its origins for granted. Our system is based upon the presumption of innocence. Sadly, we have become connected to its opposite—the presumption of guilt — and it pollutes and corrupts the essence of the American justice system.

UNDERSTANDING MIRANDA

Miranda rights are something that many people do not fully understand. Nowhere in the United States Constitution does it require any police officer to advise you of your rights. The United States Supreme Court made up the requirement in the case of *People v. Miranda*. The *Miranda* case is legendary for what many call judicial activism. Since the ruling in the *Miranda* case, officers have been advising suspects or defendants of their rights. *Miranda* only says that if you are under arrest and the cops wish to interrogate you, prior to the interrogation, they must advise you of these rights. You must waive the rights in order for your statements to be used against you.

Now, what does that actually *not* mean? It does not mean officers must advise you of your rights when they arrest you. Clients tell me, "Well, they arrested me and never read me my rights. Shouldn't the case get dropped?" *Not reading you your Miranda rights does not equal a dismissal or the inability to charge you with a crime.* Not reading your rights does not necessarily mean they violated any of your rights. Miranda means that once you are under arrest, if the officers question you, they must first advise you of your *Miranda* rights. If they fail to advise you of your rights when they question you, what you say becomes inadmissible against you, unless you contradict those statements during your testimony at trial. In other words, if you are arrested and the detective comes in to question you but he never reads you your Miranda rights, the prosecution cannot present the statements that you made against yourself in court because you were not advised of your rights. However, if you take the witness stand in your case and testify differently than what you told the detective, the prosecution can use your un-Mirandized statements to contradict you and question your honesty. For the most part, the central theme of *Miranda* is all about the statements made by a suspect while in custody and whether or not those statements are admissible in court.

The advisement pursuant to *Miranda* is: "You have the right to remain silent. Anything you say can and will be used against you in a court of law. You have a right to an attorney to be present at the time of that questioning. If you cannot afford an attorney, one will be appointed for you. Do you understand these rights?" That is the essential Miranda warning. As a matter of practice, when a person is arrested, one of the first things the officer does is Mirandize the suspect because he wants to get it out of the way. Typically, the advisement is given right away so that it's not forgotten by mistake, but there is no requirement for the officer to give the Miranda warning. Officers can arrest you and never advise you as long as they do not interrogate you.

There are many subtleties about the Miranda warning. If you are arrested but then released, when the detective calls you back and says, "Hey, sorry for the mix-up, but I want to ask you a few questions," he is not required to Mirandize you because you are sitting at home. If he comes to your house and you are both just sitting in the living room while he is interviewing you, he does not have to Mirandize you. However, if he comes to your house, puts handcuffs on you, takes you out to the patrol car, and puts you in the back of the car, then he must Mirandize you before he talks to you.

What you must remember, though, is that nothing is off the record when it comes to law enforcement officers. You do not know if they are recording your statements, and they may do so. They have the power to secretly record you. That being said, I feel that it is best for everything to be recorded because the last thing you want is the rest of your life to be subject to the frailties of another person's memory. Let's assume that the average homicide case takes 12 to 18 months to try once it has been charged. It may have taken the officer six months to investigate; therefore, before the jury trial, a homicide case may be two years old. How many other cases, how many other witnesses, and how many other people has this detective talked to during these two or three years? Do you want to rely on just his memory of the statements that you made during the initial interview that happened two or three years ago?

You want it recorded because you want to make sure that the true details of the conversation or interview are captured. Do some police officers lie? Lies are out there. There are cases of intentional dishonesty. People are people, and if they have sufficient motives, they will lie. That happens. However, more often than not, the greatest fear that any defendant should have, when it comes to the quality of the law enforcement investigation around them, is accuracy of memory. Another is the selection of words and the tone of the writing in the report, because that can change the meaning of a statement. The report's words may be accurate, but the tone and connotation may be misleading or slanted. What the defendant meant versus what is conveyed in the report's summary can be very different. I always want the whole truth, the complete statement, its details and context, so it is critical that a statement is recorded, not simply summarized in a report.

Bottom line, *nothing is off the record.* Everything you say can potentially be used against you. The officer's job is to take statements to gain evidence to prove your guilt. It is always better to have your statement recorded rather than to rely on memories that are faulty and inaccurate. It is best to invoke your right to remain silent except to request an attorney. Do not provide statements until you have had the opportunity to speak with your attorney. Your life is on the line; you want the help of an experienced criminal defense attorney who will protect your rights.

Part of re-establishing a trusting relationship with the legal system involves using all the tools the Constitution provides for you. If you don't know your rights, you need to hire a lawyer who not only knows them, but is willing to go to the mat to protect them for you. The Constitution does not just protect the rights of the guilty; it protects the rights of the innocent as well. It protects the liberty too many of us take for granted. The rights I fight to protect everyday are the great American shield against totalitarian oppression. They are the cornerstones of liberty. Modern technology can buttress these safeguards. In addition to securing the truth, requiring video recordings and audio tapes will go a long way toward restoring the public's trust in our law enforcement officers and restoring the public's trust in our judicial system.

Maybe you are a pro-cop advocate; you believe our criminal justice system is the best on earth and is inherently just. The opposite of that would mean you believe that the criminal justice system in America convicts a bunch of innocent people and targets minorities. Whatever side you're on, the fact that there are two opposite sides battling in America over how the system works speaks to the fact that there's a woeful lack of trust. Whatever the cause, whether the lack of trust is reasonable or unreasonable, whether or not one side is right or wrong, I don't care. It just tells me there's a problem and we need to fix it.

3

WHAT MAKES A GREAT CRIMINAL DEFENSE ATTORNEY?

by Stephen J. Riebling, Jr., Esq.

Stephen J. Riebling, Jr., Esq.

Riebling, Proto & Sachs, LLP
White Plains, New York
www.rpslawyers.com

Stephen J. Riebling, Jr. is a partner with the law firm of Riebling, Proto & Sachs, LLP, whose exceptional legal work has earned him recognition and praise from his many clients and members of the legal community.

Attorney Stephen J. Riebling, Jr. did his undergraduate work at the University of Richmond, Richmond, Virginia and is a graduate of Pace University School of Law in White Plains,

New York where he earned his law degree. He has, for nearly 20 years, practiced litigation and criminal defense in Federal courts as well as in the State and local courts of both New York and Connecticut from his White Plains office in Westchester County, New York.

With scores of successful jury trial verdicts and countless favorable bench decisions to his credit, attorney Riebling is well-respected among his peers for his thoughtful and effective courtroom strategies and proven litigation skills.

Attorney Riebling was named one of the top attorneys in New York by Super Lawyers Magazine, has been named to The National Trial Lawyers: Top 100 Criminal Defense Trial Lawyers, and recognized by and by being named a top attorney in the New York Metro Area by The New York Times.

WHAT MAKES A GREAT CRIMINAL DEFENSE ATTORNEY?

In our everyday lives, we do not likely give much thought to the fundamental rights and protections that our laws provide to each of us. However, that quickly changes when people find themselves under the scrutiny of law enforcement or if they are facing arrest and prosecution. When that occurs, I consider myself fortunate to be on the "front lines" to help those people protect their lives, rights, and liberties. That is one of the major reasons that I consider it a great honor to be asked to participate in this book. Not so much because I believe myself to be a great criminal defense attorney, but because my approach and philosophy, the "nuts and bolts" if you will, in defending clients both before and during trial have proven themselves to be valuable and successful assets in even the most difficult of cases. On multiple occasions, I have had other observing lawyers, opposing prosecutors, and even presiding judges approach me after trials and remark in glowing terms upon the unique way that I defended a particular case, a sentiment that my clients regularly echo.

In that regard, I have been asked repeatedly over the years to measure my successes in court by answering this question: how many trials have you won? To be frank, I stopped keeping track of that statistic a long time ago, largely due to the fact that I have encountered and opposed many prosecutors in criminal courts and attorneys in civil cases over the years who like to brag about their "winning percentages" at trial. The truth is, when I am about to begin a criminal trial, past successes, mine or theirs, have no meaning. The only thing that matters is the case at hand. Approaching every case with that singular focus and tenacity is what I would rather be known for rather than some subjective self-promoting.

That said, to be able to walk into any courtroom and know that you have the respect of your peers, the court, and, ultimately, the respect of the jury is the best way to measure success as a criminal defense attorney.

So, how do I gain their respect and translate that into success for the client? The first and most important step is preparation. Learning the facts of a case so that I can recall even the most minor detail instantly is crucial. I cannot tell you how many times I have watched an attorney lose an argument or even a trial due to the fact that they made a factual mistake. Think of it from a juror's perspective—the sole reason that they are there is to listen to testimony and remember facts. If an attorney stands up in front of them and makes factual mistakes, the juror immediately loses confidence in that attorney. Nothing is worse for a client than having a lawyer who has lost the trust of the jury.

That is a very important aspect of doing jury trials. You need to remember that trials are not like everyday life—the goal is not to be "liked." Instead, I would much rather have the respect of the jury. Think about that for a moment. You may like someone because you think that they are a nice person. You enjoy their company and like to hang out with them. However, does that automatically translate into trust? Do you believe everything that someone tells you just because they seem nice or are fun to hang out with? I would not necessarily say that. When you respect someone, when you hear them speak, you view them as authoritative. As soon as a person says, "You know what? I respect that guy. I believe what he tells me. I trust what he tells me," then they are more likely to turn to me for answers when questions arise during the trial.

When I began my career I handled only civil cases, specifically personal injury (motor vehicle accidents), products liability (when a product is claimed to be defective), and medical malpractice. It surprises many to learn this, but in my experience, the average civil case dwarfs the average criminal case in terms of the amount of information that one must review, prepare, and remember. In addition, the types of cases, in terms of fact patterns and applicable laws, are so much more varied and complex than most criminal cases. It was in these areas that I honed my techniques, developed my process of preparation, and began to think of things in different ways.

I strongly believe those experiences give me a great advantage in the criminal courts because my approach, preparation, and thought process are different from most criminal defense attorneys. Most prosecutors become prosecutors directly out of law school and are taught by prosecutors who followed the same career path. They have developed a "blueprint" or "script" as to how to do things, and it is very uncomfortable for them to vary from that script. By drawing on my experiences, where I have never had a "script" as to how to defend a case, I often approach issues from a different angle and present my case in a way that was not expected by the prosecution. This ability has resulted in many great and repeated successes for my clients over the years. This is one of the things that sets me apart from other criminal defense attorneys.

BUILDING A STRONG DEFENSE

I start building the defense of every case by looking at the criminal statute or statutes that define the crime(s) being charged. If it is an assault case, a grand larceny case, or even a murder case, I want to know exactly what the law says about each and every element (or question) that the prosecution must prove (or answer) beyond a reasonable doubt. By knowing exactly what must be established in order to prove guilt, I know exactly what issues that I need to investigate and develop. From there, I know how to steer my investigation. Often, the defense is at a disadvantage in terms of time and resources, as opposed to the prosecution that has the limitless resources and manpower of the government, so wasting time and resources on issues that will have no bearing on whether or not a client is found guilty does nothing to help my client.

However, one advantage that criminal defense attorneys have is the client. My client is usually a valuable resource that the prosecution does not have. He or she typically has a wealth of information because he or she was there. In some cases, they might be the only person, the only eyewitness, of the alleged crime. The client will often tell me, "That's not exactly how it went down." Right there, I may have an advantage over the prosecutor because I may have more information and details that will help me build the defense. The information and details from the client may also lead me to other witnesses. It is always important to speak to as many people as I can to try to gather as much information as possible. I will have an investigator speak to the same people the police have spoken to if they are available and will speak. Any statements that they are willing to give prior to trial can be helpful. However, there are always instances where witnesses for the prosecution will not speak to the investigator. In those cases, I always make it a point to ask those people when they testify how much time they spent talking to police and prosecutors in preparing their testimony. In many instances, these types of questions reveal biases against my client or a motive to lie.

In addition, the physical evidence that I review and collect is just as important as the testimony of witnesses. All photographs, videos, and any other physical evidence that has been collected by the prosecution and that they intend to use at trial must also be analyzed. Nothing is as important as knowing what the prosecution intends to offer against my client. By learning what that evidence may be, I can sometimes use that same evidence to my client's advantage. It can be very powerful and persuasive to use what the prosecution believes to be its best evidence to help prove my client's innocence.

Throughout the process of building a defense as I learn about what potential witnesses may have to say and what the physical evidence shows, I am always refining the defense. I continue to ask myself: What does the prosecution need to prove? How are they going to prove it? What are they going to use to prove their case?

Once I understand what my opponent—the prosecution—is looking to establish, then I can look for the different possibilities. Are there legal defenses that can be used? Are there statutory defenses available such as self-defense? Is there another explanation as to why the alleged event occurred? Are there other people who could have committed this crime? These are all the things that I question and review in order to build the defense.

Lastly and most importantly, I *always* keep an open mind about the case. I never know when the one detail, argument, or theory for the defense may reveal itself.

As I mentioned earlier, there is no "blueprint" to developing the defense of a criminal case. Sometimes the investigators advise me that witnesses do not have the same recollection or interpretation of the facts as originally thought. Sometimes the factual evidence leads to far different conclusions. As a result, many of my original thoughts or theories for the defense need to be abandoned or rethought. As I begin to fashion the arguments, I start to piece together the various pieces of the puzzle. Once there is a clear picture of the facts, then I can move on to the next step, how to present those facts to the jury.

Presenting the facts of a case to the jurors, the people who will determine guilt or innocence, is the ultimate test. This presentation is just as important as the facts themselves. Every case is different, so it is vital that the presentation be done in such a way that guarantees it will be received well by the jury. The presentation must be reasonable and understandable. I constantly remind myself that though I know every detail and argument inside and out, the jurors do not. They are hearing everything for the very first time, and I want them to hear the evidence in the manner that I feel is important in order to advance my defense theory.

In other words, I want to add color to the black-and-white picture that the prosecution tries to paint. I want to provide as much clarity to as possible. I want the jury to understand that this is not about checking off elements of the criminal statute. By doing this, I establish rapport with the jury, giving them reasons to trust my interpretation and presentation of the facts.

INSIDE JURY SELECTION

I would agree with the basic premise that jury selection is the most important aspect of a criminal jury trial because it is the jury that ultimately decides the fate of the client. While there are other people in the courtroom (i.e. other attorneys, judge, witnesses, etc.) who may observe the trial, my true and only audience is the jury. Selecting the right jury can mean the difference between a guilty and a non-guilty verdict.

That said, having tried many criminal jury trials, chosen many juries, and talked to many people, I can honestly say that there is no formula or trick for choosing a good jury for my client. The only way to select the best jury for my client is to sit down with each juror and get to know him or her. Before every criminal jury trial I have the opportunity to speak with the jurors, to learn about them and, by doing so, I get the first chance to develop my theories.

We all know what people say about first impressions: they are incredibly important. How I approach my client's case, how I present my client, and how I present myself is critical because jurors are interested and watching. This is the first time that they will see my client, this is the first time that they will hear me speak, and they will be formulating opinions as soon as they walk into the courtroom. Most people do not have experience with the criminal justice system, and being a juror in a criminal trial is typically the first time most people experience it. That is why a crucial part of jury selection is making the juror feel comfortable and not as though he or she is in the spotlight.

I want to have a conversation with the juror. It is not only the questions that I am asking the potential juror, but it is also the juror's reactions that I want to observe. This is the only time throughout the entire trial process that I will speak to the jurors as people, one-on-one. What I am trying to do is gauge the type of person they are and whether this person will be receptive to the defense theories and arguments during the trial. Everyone who walks into the jury room and sits in the jury box during jury selection is a potential juror. Like everyone else, they carry their own baggage in the forms of opinions and biases. As a criminal defense attorney, I need to find out what that baggage is in order to properly defend my client, because that baggage can affect the juror's decision-making process. The more I know about their background, education, and experiences can reveal a great deal about how a person will analyze information and believe arguments.

For example, if I have a case involving technical information such as blood testing, medical records, or ballistics of a gunshot, I may want jurors with a higher level of education who are more attuned to engineering and mathematics or have analytical jobs. If I have a case that involves more emotional issues, then I may want jurors who are not as technical, maybe someone who has a liberal arts background, people in the fields of education or health care who are "free thinkers."

Another element is lifestyle. Are they or have they been married? Do they have kids? If the case involves domestic violence with husbands, wives, or children, I want to find out what a juror's reaction may be to these issues. As I said, everyone walks into every situation with baggage. If I do not know what those people are thinking about, then how do I know whether they can look at the case objectively?

What else should I look for?

One issue to address is whether or not they have been a juror in other cases and if they have been party to another court proceeding. These experiences may have left lasting impressions, impressions that may affect objectivity. They may think that they know how the jury system works because they were a juror in another case. If the juror believes he or she knows the law because of a prior experience as a juror, then I need to know that. I need to determine if the juror's opinions or thoughts can be changed and if the juror is receptive to different possibilities. If the juror is not receptive, then that juror may not be the best person to be on the jury for my case.

The more questions asked, the more is learned about each juror. As a criminal defense attorney, I will always talk about the burden of proof. Making sure the juror understands that the prosecution has the burden of proving someone's guilt beyond a reasonable doubt is an absolute must. Criminal defendants do not have that burden under the law. Jurors must not hold this against the client and they must not require the client to put on a case, because the law does not require the client to do so. Any juror who cannot accept this aspect of the law should not be sitting on any criminal trial.

I always talk with jurors about the importance of having an open mind. They must have an open mind from the moment they sit in the jury box. I want to make sure that people will not make decisions along the way. As human beings we have a habit of jumping to conclusions and making rash decisions as soon as we hear something. Jurors must understand what is expected of them. They cannot allow their baggage and pre-conceptions about things to color their judgments and impair their decision-making in a criminal trial. They cannot pre-judge a case. Every juror must understand that it may be the last thing that they hear from the last witness, the last piece of physical evidence that they review, or even the last argument made by one of the attorneys that can be the most important piece of the puzzle. If they do not keep an open mind throughout, then they can miss or even disregard something important.

Ultimately, when it comes down to jury selection, the jurors select themselves. This is something I have heard many people say and something that I subscribe to because it is a juror's answers, how a juror responds, how open a juror is, and how honest a juror wants to be that determines whether the juror is a good fit for the particular case.

With that in mind, jurors will often say or do things during the jury selection that give us a reason to challenge them and ask that they be removed from the jury panel. These types of challenges are called "cause challenges." Cause challenges are brought to the attention of the judge and the judge will determine if the juror is or is not a good fit for this particular case.

In some cases, I just get a feeling about a potential juror. Maybe they said or reacted in a particular way to something I said, maybe something in their past experiences leads me to think that they will not be a good juror for my client. In those instances, I may use statutory challenges or peremptory challenges to excuse a potential juror from the jury panel.

At the conclusion of jury selection, I want to be able to look at the jurors selected and turn to my client and say, "This is the group of people who will be the most open and receptive to your case." As I said at the beginning of this section, choosing the right jury may be the most important part of the trial because the jury is the audience and they will decide the fate of the client.

MAKING A STRONG OPENING STATEMENT

The opening statement is the first time that I have the opportunity to stand in front of the audience (the jury) and present my theory of the case. Over the years, I have seen many attorneys make a critical tactical error by misconstruing the opening statement as only a general "statement" of things they intend to prove and then they go on to systematically list a series of facts involved with the case. I like to think about the opening statement in this context: there are only two times once the trial actually begins when an attorney may directly address a jury. First is during opening statements and second is during closing arguments. From my perspective, I do not want to waste an opportunity to develop my theory of the defense. So, my goal is to not only tell the jury about the crucial facts, but I also want them to begin viewing those facts in the manner that I feel is important to my theory of the defense. At the very beginning, I fashion the opening statement in order to set the tone, focus the jurors on what issues are important to my client's case, and establish trust with the jury.

Since the opening statement is so vital to the defense, I always make sure I know exactly what I want to say and I am careful to rehearse the opening statement so that the words become second nature. The words that I use, the way that I use them, how I stand, and how I move is important. It is not just what I am saying to the jury, it is how I deliver those words. I want to convey conviction and belief with both my statements and my body language.

This does not necessarily mean that I stand in front of the jury with a closed fist and bang on the table. That would be confusing emotion with conviction. Conviction means conveying how much I believe in what the evidence will show. At the start of the trial, I am establishing trust with the jurors so that they will look to me as the teller of truth and the source of accurate facts.

With that in mind, I am not a strong believer in long, drawn-out introductions at the start of opening statements, where I remind them of who I am and thank them for their service. I find those types of beginnings to be forced and disingenuous. If the jury does not know who I am and whom I represent from jury selection, then something is already terribly wrong. I prefer to launch directly into my case. I want to capture them immediately and tell them the most important part of the case in the first few minutes. Like most people, jurors want to be engaged immediately or they will lose interest in what I am saying. That is why I want to deliver the most important aspect of my case and what I intend to do while I have their complete attention. I want to set the mood right off the bat. My impact statement is specifically tailored and designed to grab their attention with a powerful, gripping account or statement of facts.

Some lawyers believe that they should not make arguments to the jury during opening statements. I guess in a technical sense they are correct; after all, they are called "opening statements." However, I do not subscribe to that technical definition. There is absolutely no reason that I should not start the case by arguing my theories to the jury, establishing the framework for my arguments and the conclusions that I want them to draw from the evidence.

Many studies show that cases are won during the opening statement. That is something that I want to take advantage of as soon as possible.

I always like to tell the jury right at the beginning the questions I want them to answer. I do not want them to speculate about the issues that I see as important. In the opening statement, I tell them, "These are the questions you should be asking yourselves as you hear this case." I also tell them what the answers to those questions are going to be based on the evidence that they will see. Again, I do not want them to be unclear as to my client's position.

There is one danger that many people fall into during the opening statement; that is over-promising things to the jury. It is very easy to over-promise during the opening statement. It is critically important that I only promise what I know I can deliver throughout the trial. If I over-promise and it does not play out the way that I promised, then my opponent will surely point it out to the jury, causing me to lose credibility in the eyes of the jury, and this could result in my client getting convicted. I never want to be in the position where opposing counsel says, "Remember when Mr. Riebling told you at the beginning of this case that he would prove this fact? Well, he did not keep his promise!"

So, do not oversell the case during the opening statement. Only sell what can be provided, and sell it with passion and conviction. I want the jury to go through the trial seeing things as the defense sees them. If I do not convince the jury in the opening to start down that path with me, it will be much more difficult for me to raise questions that ultimately convince the jury to find my client not guilty when I close the case.

CROSS-EXAMINATION — EXPOSING THE TRUTH FROM FICTION

When we think of cross-examination, we likely conjure up thoughts of things we have seen on television or in the movies. The truth about cross-examination is that it is often not as dramatic as we think. My goals during cross-examination are simple: I want to "score points" and raise questions about the "truthfulness" of the witness.

First, what do I mean by "scoring points"? Well, whenever a witness takes the stand for the prosecution, the assumption is that the witness will only provide information to help the prosecution's case. That is a mistake. Any witness that takes the stand has the potential of providing information that is beneficial for the defense. The trick is knowing what information to get from which witness and how. Often, the prosecution's witnesses do not even know that the information they are providing is benefiting the defendant until it is too late. As such, they are more than willing to provide the facts that I am eliciting. Why would I want to elicit the testimony from a prosecution witness rather than just a defense witness? The answer is simple: it gives more credibility to the arguments that I intend to make at closing argument on behalf of the defendant. Nothing is more powerful and more convincing than having people who are called on behalf of the prosecution to suddenly start offering facts and agreeing with the statements of the defense attorney. In my closing, I then remind the jurors of the testimony and use it to the advantage of my client.

The important thing about "scoring points" with the prosecution's witnesses is to recognize when to stop and to get out while I am ahead. In other words, my goal with any witness is to address a maximum of three to four key issues or facts that will further my arguments later during closing arguments.

In all my years of practice, there have been only a handful of times where a witness has completely collapsed under cross-examination and provided testimony that on its own could "win" the case. Since it happens so rarely, it should never be the goal of cross-examination to try and elicit such testimony. I have seen far too many lawyers try to do this and often they end up arguing with the witness, getting testimony that they do not want, and losing credibility in the eyes of the jury.

The second goal that I mentioned for cross-examination is questioning the "truthfulness" of a witness. In this situation, my goal during cross-examination is to separate the truth of what they are saying from potential exaggeration or embellishment—what I like to call "creative truth telling." People are prone to make mistakes and have faulty recollections. Perceptions are easily distorted and confused. As such, people are prone to changing their story, to filling in the blanks in their memory with things that they believe happened instead of what actually happened. That is where the prepared criminal defense attorney can develop reasonable doubt.

I often tell jurors in my closing argument: If a person is telling the truth, they should tell us the same thing each time they recount their story. If facts begin to change over time, then that indicates they are not being truthful to us. As a defense attorney, I want to expand and highlight those types of inconsistencies in front of the jury during the course of my cross-examination.

As there is no shortcut, formula, or standard question that everyone can rely on for cross-examination of a witness. The real key to good or even great cross-examination is preparation and experience.

If I am prepared and organized, I will begin to sense when the witness is starting to feel the pressure of my questions. There have been times when I have actually seen a witness come to the realization that the answers they have given have "boxed them in" and that the ultimate question, the most important question, can only be answered in one way—the way I want them to answer it.

How do I start this process?

First, I do the homework. Review prior statements or testimony that they have given. Know the facts of the case; make the witnesses agree to the facts and things that make common sense. No one wants to look unreasonable on the witness stand.

Second, I listen to their direct testimony. I always listen intently to what they say throughout the direct examination. Sometimes a witness will go on and on and on, but what he or she says has not added to the prosecution's case. So, as I listen, I ask myself: Have they said anything that is materially against my client? Have they injured my client's case or my client's innocence in any way? If they have, then I will explore what they said. Have they made any other statements? Have they said things that just do not make sense? Is there other evidence available to me that I can use to expose their lack of truth or their exaggeration? If so, I will use all of those weapons against them and expose their faulty memory, exaggerations, or even lies.

Do I cross-examine every witness? Many times, I look at the witness, stand up, and tell the court that I do not have a single question. When I cross-examine a witness, I do not do so just for the sake of asking questions. I must have a point. What am I trying to accomplish, what is my agenda?

Remember, I want to score points. I want to expose any "creativity" that may have crept into their testimony. I want to expose their exaggeration, expose any false testimony, and create doubt in the minds of the jurors.

Depending on where an attorney practices, the rules may or may not permit them to take testimony from witness prior to trial. In all jurisdictions, a defense attorney, to the extent possible, should interview witnesses and obtain statements. Those statements can be used very effectively at trial. Any written statements a witness may have given to the police, any statement that I may be able to get from them during the course of my own investigation, or anything else they might have told other people can be used to highlight inconsistencies. This is a gold mine for a defense attorney because it gives something with which to attack the witness's credibility and testimony while they are on the witness stand.

Prior to a witness taking the witness stand, it is likely that I will have at least a general idea of what they are going to say based on other materials I have in front of me. Unfortunately, I do not have a crystal ball, and thus I will never know the actual words that a witness will use until they speak. What witnesses may utter or how they may actually describe something or react to something—those are things I won't know until I am in the courtroom.

Therefore, a criminal defense attorney should not be prepared just for the issues that he wants to explore but also for the topics that just pop up during the course of the direct examination. Sometimes the way a witness chooses their words or what they intentionally omit from their answer can result in great material for cross-examination. For example, I had a case a couple of years ago where an expert for the prosecution was on the stand. During his direct testimony, he outlined in detail and with great care those items that he reviewed and relied upon in formulating his opinions. However, he quickly glossed over a few items that contained information essential to the case. On its face, it could have appeared innocent. However, it occurred to me that he never reviewed the reports that were necessary in order for him to reach certain conclusions. The clue was in the subtle way he answered the questions about those reports. Under cross-examination I discovered that he had not reviewed those specific records and reports.

Additionally, I revealed that instead of relying on those necessary documents, he relied on the summary information and conclusions provided by the prosecutor. Needless to say, the cross-examination went a long way towards discrediting the expert's testimony and it all stemmed from me noticing a minor omission in the testimony, recognizing the importance of that omission, and being prepared to take immediate advantage of it as soon as I had my chance to question him. Situations like that make all the difference. The lesson: it is vitally important that a criminal defense attorney pay close attention to the way a witness answers each question, as it could be crucial to the case.

THE CLOSING ARGUMENT — PUTTING ALL OF THE PIECES TOGETHER

Closing arguments afford me the opportunity to pull all the evidence together and make the case for my client. It is the part of the trial that I have been building towards the entire time. I get to review with the jurors all of the facts that they have been listening to for days or weeks. Most importantly, I get to tell them how they should interpret those facts and what conclusions they must draw.

How I frame my closing argument depends on the theory of the case. When I am arguing that the prosecution did not prove guilt beyond a reasonable doubt, I show why the evidence does not support a conclusion of guilt. However, the trick is not to just make a blanket statement regarding the position. I want to play to the jury's sense of reasoning. Using the evidence, I like to "help" the jurors arrive at the conclusion that I want them to draw from the facts. When appropriate, a defense attorney should highlight why the evidence shows something different from what the prosecution is arguing. If a reasonable alternative explanation can be reached viewing the same evidence from a different perspective, then it needs to be explained in great detail.

I always like to draw on the facts and arguments that I mentioned in my opening. It helps to bring continuity and even credibility to the closing. In particular, it is necessary to show the jury that those things I promised during the opening have been established by the evidence. For example, I want to be able to tell the jury, "I told you that a witness would give testimony saying this and swearing that. I told you the prosecution would not be able to produce this important piece of evidence." Now, at the close of the case, I will remind the jurors, "I told you this would or would not happen and, based on everything that I laid out for you in the opening statement, this should be the outcome."

More often than not, these types of sensible and rational arguments, appealing to a person's common sense, resonate and lead people to believe what they are being told.

Regardless of the defense theory, it is important to be very frank and honest with the jury. I always remind them of the questions I asked them to ask themselves in my opening statement. Since those questions are usually based on the law that they are going to hear from the judge, it is important that they know from me how the evidence supports the answers that I want them arrive at. For example, if it is an assault case, I will say, "Ask yourselves, did the prosecution prove beyond a reasonable doubt that my client had the intent to cause serious physical injury?" Then, in great detail, I will go over the evidence with them so that they understand why the answer to that question must be "no." We arrive at the answer to the question together, using the evidence as support and appealing to reason and the common sense of the jury.

As I have said throughout, there is no "blueprint" that I follow, and every case that I defend must be looked at differently, as every case has its own unique set of facts and issues. While the prosecution generally deals with things in black and white, I always want to establish the theory of my defense by providing "color" in the form of context and detail. Using the facts of the case, reason, and common sense, I want to help the jurors fill in the blanks, answer unanswered questions, raise reasonable doubt, and/or establish an alternative theory as to how or why something occurred.

All great defense attorneys live to do this—it's what makes them successful. It's what makes them great.

(This content should be used for informational purposes only. It does not create an attorney-client relationship with any reader and should not be construed as legal advice. If you need legal advice, please contact an attorney in your community who can assess the specifics of your situation.)

4

WHO WILL DEFEND YOU?

by Carmen Gosselin, Esq.

Carmen Gosselin, Esq.
C.G. Law PLLC
Phoenix, Arizona
www.cglawpllc.com

Carmen Gosselin grew up in the suburbs of Detroit, Michigan where, some would say, Gosselin showed a penchant for challenging authority from a very early age. She earned her Bachelor of Arts in Philosophy from Arizona State University. She went on to study and to earn her law degree at the Sandra Day O'Connor College of Law.

Gosselin lives and practices in Phoenix, Arizona, where she specializes in criminal defense cases. She was recently featured in Attorney at Law Magazine in their series, "Lawyers to Watch in 2015."

The counselor enjoys her specialty but finds it most fulfilling when she can use her skills to protect the rights of individuals in trouble. In her perfect world, fairness and justice would trump politics in the courtroom. Ms. Gosselin's goal; "...change the system to be less about re-election and retribution, and more about rehabilitation."

WHO WILL DEFEND YOU?

When a person is arrested and later charged with a crime, the entire focus of his (or her) world instantly changes. Most people facing this situation are overwhelmed and do not know where to begin. If you find yourself in this situation, the first and most important step to take is to speak with a lawyer. Depending on your financial situation, you may qualify for a public defender. However, you will not have any choice in deciding which public defender ultimately represents you. If you want the ability to choose a lawyer, you will have to hire a private attorney. And remember, you have a right to hire an attorney, even on the eve of trial. So if you feel your lawyer is not providing the level of attention that your case requires, you need to hire someone new.

Now, when you decide to hire a lawyer, it is important to remember that he or she is the person who will be your voice in court. You need to choose carefully. Just because you are paying a private attorney does not necessarily mean that you are getting a better attorney. I believe the most important thing to consider when hiring a lawyer is whether the attorney understands your desired outcome and is then able to communicate her plan to achieve it. An attorney's ability to do this largely depends on whether he or she has the time available to actually listen to all of your concerns.

One of the common complaints heard from court-appointed attorneys is the enormous case load placed on their shoulders. The sheer number of clients does not allow the time required to adequately listen to every single client's concerns. On the other hand, a good private attorney should be able to offer immediate counseling and peace of mind to every single client. As a private attorney, I control my own caseload, which allows me to offer the kind of one-on-one attention required to address and reassure my clients regarding their concerns.

After you have made the decision to hire an attorney, your next step is to find her. One of the first places you should start is on the Internet. A good search for an attorney who may specialize in the kind of crime with which you've been charged could help narrow down your choices. For example, if you have been charged with DUI, find an attorney with substantial experience in DUI law. But always remember that much of what you can read online is part of business advertising, so read with a careful eye.

The Internet is a great resource, but it can only get you so far depending on where you look. Your state bar association will have useful information so be sure to check out its website. Also, there are some websites, like Avvo, that actually have a rating system for lawyers with photographs and client reviews. Take your time, check multiple websites, and you should be able to find the very best attorney that you can afford.

Another useful tool when looking for a good lawyer is good old-fashioned word-of-mouth referrals, or referrals from friends or relatives. Word-of-mouth referrals are still the gold standard in advertising, and that is true with attorney referrals.

If the internet or a word-of-mouth referral does not satisfy you, you can always go to court and sit through the morning calendar. Doing this will give you an opportunity to watch different attorneys interact with their clients, the prosecutor, and the court. Watching how a lawyer behaves in court can tell you a lot about how she may interact with you.

Unfortunately, if you are in custody, you will not be able to access the internet or simply show up to morning court. Under those circumstances, you will have to rely on friends and family to hire an attorney for you. But is important to know that the sooner your family retains an attorney, the sooner a lawyer will start working on your case. This seems like an obvious statement, but a court-appointed attorney typically does not have the time to take immediate action on a case that has just been assigned to him. Therefore, you may be waiting for some time before he can meet with you, let alone start working on any part of your case, including your release from jail.

Whether you or your family is in the process of hiring an attorney these tips are important to remember: 1) Does the attorney have prior experience with your type of case? 2) Is the attorney listening to your concerns and communicating a plan of action? 3) Does the attorney have adequate time required to start working on your case immediately?

COST CONSIDERATIONS

A good criminal defense attorney can ultimately save you thousands of dollars in criminal penalties and fines. A lawyer who knows and fully understands the collateral financial consequences for the crime you are charged with is worth her weight in gold. For example, a DUI conviction will also result in Motor Vehicle Department fines and fees, car insurance consequences, and court imposed treatment costs. If an attorney does not know about these consequences, it is unlikely that he will consider them when negotiating a plea agreement, which could be detrimental to your finances. A good attorney will consider all of these expenses when proceeding with plea negotiations and hopefully minimize any financial risks. Furthermore, if you hire a criminal defense attorney at the beginning of the case, this decision could end up saving you thousands of dollars later. In some situations, your lawyer may be able to maneuver around and avoid costly requirements or work out a plea agreement that will not require you to pay those fines and fees later on.

Another important aspect of cost consideration is to determine what actual services are included in the cost. For example, a privately hired attorney may include representation on issues that an appointed attorney simply will not cover. For example, I include representation at the MVD administrative hearing related to a DUI charge, whereas a court-appointed attorney will not include this type of representation because it does not involve the "criminal" case. Without getting into too much detail, knowing the consequences of fighting and winning or fighting and losing a MVD hearing could potentially save you thousands of dollars in the long run.

AN ADVERSARIAL SYSTEM

The justice system in the United States of America is an adversarial system and, while it can be improved, it is still the best system in the world today.

Adversarial simply means that when you go to court, you and your lawyer face off against the prosecution, whose job is to convict you (ethically speaking, the prosecutor's job is to uphold justice but this seems to be forgotten at times). The prosecutor, with the help of the police, will try to convict you of the crime with which you are charged.

On your side is the Constitution, which guarantees your right to an attorney. If you do not have the money to hire an attorney, an attorney should be appointed to you (as long as you are facing a charge that could result in potential jail sentence). Whether you hire an attorney or are appointed one, you should never proceed on your own. I would never recommend that you go to court without a lawyer.

If you had a leak in your roof, it is usually a better idea to call a professional roofer than to try to fix it yourself. Similarly, it is usually a better idea to call a lawyer, and the sooner the better. Hiring a lawyer can provide peace of mind by way of the one-on-one direct attention your case deserves. It usually will take longer to get in touch with the court-appointed attorney, which inevitably will cause people to get nervous; just dealing with the anxiety of waiting to talk to an attorney can be excruciating all by itself. Because you are usually unfamiliar with the process, you absolutely should not proceed with any aspect of your case without talking to an attorney first.

It is truly important to remember that a great number of serious mistakes can be made, which might never be undone, when you try to take on your adversaries alone.

PROTECTING YOURSELF FROM THE ADVERSARIES

Protecting yourself from your adversaries is probably THE most essential part of your criminal case. When you are charged with a crime, your adversary is the prosecutor who will determine which charges you will face; try not to lend him a hand. A good prosecutor will read the police report, and determine charges based on what he reads. A police officer may cite you for numerous offenses, but that does not mean that the prosecutor will go forward with charging those offenses. The prosecutor has the discretion to ascertain what offense will ultimately be charged.

Unfortunately, the prosecutor's decision will be based on just a one-sided story of the event. The prosecutor's office will not call you or any other witnesses to describe what happened.

At this point, there is probably nothing that you can do to help your case, unless the police do want to talk to you during an ongoing investigation. On the other hand, there are many, many ways that you can harm your case. If the police do want to talk to you and there is an ongoing investigation, I always recommend that you *never talk to the police—or be interviewed on the phone—without an attorney present*. Phone calls are recorded, and interviews can be recorded.

Remember, though unfair, police are permitted to lie. It's legal for them to tell you, "Just come in and talk to us. It'll be no big deal," when in fact, they're interrogating you and will use what you say against you in their reports. If there's an ongoing investigation and that report hasn't yet been submitted to the prosecutor, it's not in your best interests to speak with anyone without an attorney present, because the prosecutor will look at the officer's report in determining your charges.

In terms of helping your case, the police do have some discretion; a good police officer will use that discretion by fully investigating the case. No doubt, he will have questions for you. Nevertheless, I would never recommend direct contact with the police. I would always recommend that you hire an attorney to help you maintain contact with the police. Once the police officer submits the police report to the prosecutor for charging, there is really nothing that you can do.

WHO IS PROSECUTING?

Simply put, prosecutors are overworked. It is critical to understand that it does not matter whether the prosecutor is brand-new or well-seasoned; there is not enough time in the day for him to be 100 percent prepared, updated, and fully informed about each assigned case. Consequently, the duty to inform the prosecutor of the weakness of your case rests with your defense attorney. In my experience, it is rare to have a prosecutor show up to court and immediately know everything there is to know about your case and your situation. For those reasons, you need an attorney who has a good working relationship with the prosecutor's office or at least the ability to work with the office to be able to adequately convey the weaknesses of the case and circumstances specifically related to you.

In most situations, a good defense attorney will inform the prosecutor about all of the nuances of your case, the law, and the facts that may be exculpatory or helpful to you and your defense, especially when trying to negotiate a favorable pre-trial outcome. In my experience, a prosecutor will use a usually make a superficial assessment of the case when determining a plea offer. So it is usually my responsibility to provide the detailed information that helps my client get a better plea. On the other hand, if a case is on track to proceed to trial, then any lack of preparation on the prosecutor's part is always beneficial.

The three most important things to remember about your prosecutor: 1) a court will not change the prosecutor on your case under almost all circumstances, 2) the prosecutor rarely cares about your particular circumstances prior to your lawyer informing him about said circumstances, and 3) a prosecutor is typically concerned with getting a conviction and not with "helping" you.

FELONY VS. MISDEMEANOR

The difference between a felony and a misdemeanor comes down to the seriousness of the charge and the resulting punishment that goes along with that. A misdemeanor charge, in the State of Arizona, can range from a Class 1 to a Class 3 misdemeanor. Felony charges are much more serious charges; they range from Class 6 to Class 2 (Class 1 felony is first-degree murder). For a felony charge, you are probation-eligible for your first offense but the court could impose prison time, whereas a misdemeanor charge could include probation and up to 6 months in jail. The jail is typically run by either the county sheriff or the city authorities, whereas prison is run by the State's Department of Corrections.

Other differences include those which can be used against you in future criminal cases. In the State of Arizona, a felony can be used against you (depending on when it occurred and when you were convicted), either as a historical or non-historical prior, increasing any future punishments you may face. A felony can also have greater collateral consequences in that you may have to admit to the conviction on a job application or rental application. Typically, misdemeanors are much less serious and have less collateral consequences than felony convictions.

MIRANDA RIGHTS (OR WARNINGS)

An officer is required to inform you of your Miranda Rights after you have been detained or arrested and before any interrogation. To determine whether the police violated your Miranda rights you must ask yourself two questions: 1) Was the police officer not allowing me to leave? 2) Was the police officer asking me incriminating questions? If the answer to *both* of these questions is yes, then you may have a substantial legal issue.

If the officer does not give you proper notice of your Miranda Rights, then any incriminating statements may be inadmissible in court. Many times, people think that their rights have been violated or their case should be dismissed because the officer didn't read the Miranda Rights, but they only protect against any incriminating statements that you make. So, the police officer who doesn't ask you any incriminating questions doesn't have to read you the Miranda Rights, especially if you do not make any incriminating statements.

According to the police, people confess all the time. Be aware that the police know the law. When we read police reports, they are often seeded with phrases like this: "He excitedly uttered, 'I did the crime. I shoplifted. I put it in my pocket.'" Since police officers know that an "excited uttering" doesn't protect the suspect, they will attempt to code their reports to disadvantage you as much as possible.

It is important that you tell your attorney exactly what happened and what was said. Even if your account does match the police report, there still could be underlying issues to explore.

CONFESSIONS

Attorneys hear this from time to time: "I confessed when I got arrested. I was nervous and didn't know what to do. Does this mean I'm automatically guilty?"

No, it does not mean you're automatically guilty. There are numerous peer-reviewed scientific studies regarding coerced confessions. These studies cover the reasons a person who is innocent—who didn't commit the crime—would confess to that crime. One of the reasons is nervousness, but there are a lot of other possible reasons. Just because you confessed to the crime does not mean that you're automatically guilty.

The police are trained in interrogation; they are allowed to lie to you, but they are not allowed to make promises or threats. That's why defense attorneys frequently want to obtain a copy of the recorded interview or interrogation of the defendant, because there could be evidence of promises, threats, or coercion. If a person has been arrested, he will be nervous — he is anxious and fearful. A trained interrogator can make veiled promises or veiled threats that a defense attorney will be able to point out. The defense attorney will also try to get those statements dismissed before the trial.

As an accused person, you were under a great deal of pressure in a bad situation. Just because you may think that you confessed to a crime, doesn't necessarily mean that you actually did confess, or that a jury will ever hear that confession. This is also an important point to raise in pre-negotiations. If the confession was obtained in an unlawful way, the attorney can say, "Hey, we've looked at the interview. There was x promise and y promise and z threat. No judge will allow his confession admitted at trial."

HONESTY AS A POLICY?

Honesty is generally a really great policy but maybe not the best policy in criminal defense cases.

You might say, "Hey, I'm totally innocent. I'm just going to be honest. I'll talk to whoever, whenever, about whatever they want to know." Remember: at all times, the State is there to convict you. The police are there to investigate the crime. They want to close a case and they are allowed to lie. There can be veiled promises and veiled threats. They're trying to get you to confess. I don't want to say that all police are out there to get you, but in my experience, complete honesty is almost never the best policy.

The best policy is to have your attorney present to talk with the police. It is important to have your attorney present because your word can be twisted and changed, especially if there is no unbiased person there recording or witnessing the actual event. Honesty may not be the best policy when people are free to interpret what you are saying, distorting your "truth" into a completely different version of events.

PRESERVING THE EVIDENCE

Take a moment to think about the many places nowadays with cameras that are constantly recording. You can think of those videos as witnesses that can make all the difference in your case. However, people do not often realize that those videos are not stored forever. Typically, the footage is recorded over on some type of schedule. In some instances, a store will have a 30-day loop, meaning your video will only be available for 30 days. Some places only have a seven-day loop so that video will only remain safely accessible for seven days. Because police do not always fully investigate a crime, they do not necessarily retrieve the video of the alleged crime. The longer that it takes to request the video, the bigger the chance exists that it was already destroyed.

The sooner that you hire an attorney, the sooner she can try to get that video, or at least ask that the video be preserved until they can get a subpoena for the video as evidence. I cannot tell you how many times or in how many cases that my client has told me, "The video will show that I did not do what the police officer says I did," only to find that the video has been destroyed. Preserving evidence is critically important early in your case — the earlier the better.

A common mistake is to believe that if the police did not preserve the video, then your case should simply be dismissed. Unfortunately, the law (at least in Arizona) does not always work out that way. Here, unless the police acted in bad faith in the destruction of the video, your case will proceed. For an example, let's say that the officer got the video, watched it, said, "This is terrible," and destroyed it. If that happened, then your case might be dismissed. If the officer just failed to go back and retrieve the video, then he was merely negligent. At that point, the court will likely not dismiss your case, but if you proceed to trial, the judge may instruct the jury that they can consider the fact that police were negligent in the destruction of the surveillance video which can create reasonable doubt.

Thus, the judge merely informs the jury that they may consider that fact, but the jury at that point is asked to consider a great many things. That is why it is important to hire an attorney to help you preserve the video before the damage is done. A good attorney will have what is known as a preservation letter ready to go in such situations.

POLICE MISCONDUCT

In recent history, cases involving police brutality have been appearing in the news. Proving police misconduct is usually a difficult task for any attorney. It is difficult because people have a natural inclination to believe a police officer is there to help, not to hurt. It is much easier to overcome this bias when you have an eyewitness to that misconduct. If you are involved in any type of incident involving police misconduct, then you must be proactive.

Eyewitnesses may still be near the scene. Video surveillance may still be available. The best defense starts immediately after you are arrested. If you are unable to gather the evidence yourself, then you must hire a lawyer with the ability gather it for you.

GETTING ARRESTED AND CHARGED

Once you are arrested, either a summons in the mail or a ticket, the citation will tell you all of the key details: court, time, and location. For most jurisdictions, you can go online to access court records and find out the location and name of your court, and the name of your assigned judge.

If you are arrested, the process depends upon the seriousness of your charges. Typically, after arrest, you are either released and given a citation or seen by a judge within 24 hours. A judge will inform you of the charges you are facing and then impose release conditions. In most situations, you are not going to be held in jail without some sort or bond.

If you are held in jail and a bond is imposed. You will have to come up with the funds in order to be released. If you are not able to post bail, then you will definitely have to utilize friends and family to help you find an attorney or get in touch with the public defender assigned to your case. In my experience, a private attorney is going to be able to work on getting your bond reduced or modifying your release conditions much sooner than a court-appointed attorney.

TO PLEAD OR NOT TO PLEAD

Whether to take a plea bargain or go to trial, is highly fact-specific. You need an attorney to review your charges and the facts of the case. A good attorney will fully explain the outcome of the plea bargain versus the outcome of a trial conviction. Although it may be unpleasant, your attorney should always inform you of the worst-case scenario. You do not want an attorney with rose colored glasses who simply glosses over any uncomfortable possibilities. You need all the information to make an informed decision.

Even if you are completely innocent of the charges (which, sadly, happens much more often than you may think), you might still believe it is safer to enter a plea bargain than face the consequences of a trial conviction. To say that this is an unfortunate crossroad is an understatement. This type of dilemma is a result of harsh mandatory sentencing laws and the decline of judicial autonomy but it is a reality that exists and one that must be dealt with.

To enter a plea bargain, you have to admit a factual basis for the charge to which you are pleading guilty. So if you are innocent of the charged crime but your version of the facts includes some other violation of the law, a good attorney may be able to negotiate that the prosecutor amend the charge and allow you to plead guilty to the crime you will admit to committing rather than the crime you were charged with, which can be especially helpful if the amended version is a lesser crime or carries a more lenient penalty. The following is an example.

You are charged with assault, but there is a valid self-defense or mutual combat argument. Unfortunately, you have a prior conviction and risk prison time if you are convicted at trial. The State refuses to dismiss the assault charge. But you hired a good lawyer and, after speaking with you about the case, she determined that you were yelling that night and you did, in fact, disturb the peace and quiet of the lady who lived across the street who called 911. Realizing that there is a factual basis to plead guilty to the charge of disorderly conduct, your lawyer convinces the prosecutor to amend the charge and allow you to plead guilty to the lesser charge. The State still end up with your conviction and you end up on probation instead of facing a prison sentence.

Other reasons you might consider when entering into a plea bargain rather than going to trial include the bias associated with the specific crime for which you're charged, the unwillingness of the prosecutor to engage in pre-trial negotiations, or the dynamics of the jury pool in your jurisdiction. All of these factors must be considered as part of the risk analysis when deciding whether to enter a plea bargain or go to trial.

You will also need to consider any collateral consequences. For instance, if you're facing a DUI, some questions that need to be considered are, "Will your license be suspended and for how long? What will the Motor Vehicle Department require from you in order to get your license back—an ignition-interlock-device or a large reinstatement fee?" And DUIs are not the only crimes with collateral consequences. For those reasons, it is extremely important that you ask your attorney the right questions and that your attorney informs you about possible collateral consequences you may face upon entering the plea. You want to be prepared and not surprised by some unknown detail prior to entering the plea because it is very difficult to "get out" of the plea once it is entered and accepted by the court.

Important things to remember when deciding to enter a plea or not: 1) What is the difference between the plea bargain and trial conviction? 2) What obstacles do I have to overcome to win at trial? 3) What is the worst case scenario I will have to face if I am convicted at trial including any collateral consequences?

PREPARING FOR TRIAL

In preparing for trial, most of the work rests upon your attorney. Your attorney will have to interview all the witnesses, visit the crime scene, physically examine the evidence, interview witnesses, and so on. Your case may require experts who will review the evidence. Your attorney must also prepare any witnesses who will testify on your behalf. Preparing a witness involves an examination of his testimony, and maybe even a mock cross-examination to ensure no one is surprised by the process when called to testify. Trial and cross-examination can be a nerve-wracking ordeal. Testifying in court in front of a jury can be a very intimidating circumstance for some people, so it is definitely a good idea to prepare you and/or your witnesses to be comfortable while testifying.

Preparing for trial is extraordinarily time-consuming. At times, you may feel like nothing is really being accomplished. However, behind the scenes, there are details, logistics, and preparations taking place to ensure everything goes smoothly in the courtroom. This is where your attorney spends countless hours working on your case because everything must appear effortless in court.

CONCLUSION

A good attorney will know the specifics of your case, talk to witnesses, and even visit the scene. She will inform the prosecutor about the weaknesses of the case and, ultimately, get the best resolution possible. Your attorney should provide you the one-on-one attention your case and your peace-of-mind requires.

Whether you hire an attorney or are appointed one, that attorney should know the facts of your case and have a clear strategy on how to help you. Either way, you absolutely need a lawyer as soon as possible in order to navigate the unknown.

The bottom line is that you need an attorney who can devote some time to your case. Yes, it may cost you some money. On the other hand, if that attorney can get you acquitted or have your case dismissed, it is absolutely worthwhile in the long run. Call in a professional as soon as possible in order to preserve the evidence and protect you—from yourself *and* your adversaries.

(This content should be used for informational purposes only. It does not create an attorney-client relationship with any reader and should not be construed as legal advice. If you need legal advice, please contact an attorney in your community who can assess the specifics of your situation.)

5

THE PLAY'S THE THING!

by Alex Foster, Esq.

Alex Foster, Esq.
Law Office of Alex Foster, LLC
Rockville, Maryland
www.alexfosterlaw.com

Alex Foster was a professional actor for seven years before going to law school. He appeared on numerous daytime television serials including, "One Live To Live," "Search For Tomorrow," "As The World Turns," "Another World," and "Ryan's Hope." He is a graduate of Emory University School of Law in Atlanta, Georgia. In law school, he finished first (out of 300 competitors) in the school's Moot Court competition and represented Emory in the National Moot Court competition.

Alex Foster then served for 20 years as an Assistant State's Attorney for the Montgomery County State's Attorney's Office. There, he tried over one hundred jury trials, focusing on cases of homicide, child abuse, sexual assault and animal cruelty. He now practices criminal law in Rockville, Maryland where he utilizes the skills he learned as both an actor and a prosecutor to defend those charged with serious crimes.

THE PLAY'S THE THING!

When I speak to students planning to attend law school, they often ask me, "What should I study in college?" When I advise, "Theater," the response is usually one of surprise. I might hear a smirk or perhaps a giggle; they were expecting me to say Economics, History, or English. While my suggestion may seem trite, based upon my nearly 30 years of experience as a prosecutor and defense attorney, I know, unquestionably, it is true. Theater is the ultimate blend of performance, public speaking, and storytelling. Learning these skills—how to be comfortable getting up on your feet and presenting a story, how to advocate and speak convincingly, how to effectively *persuade*—these are the essential tools of the trade required to become a winning defense attorney, prosecutor, or courtroom litigator.

My life goal in high school (other than to play basketball for the New York Knicks!) was to be a great Shakespearean stage actor. I went to a performing arts college and graduated with a Theater Arts degree. I spent seven years before law school as a professional actor, appearing in stage productions and dozens of daytime soap opera episodes. I've had voice and movement lessons. I went to law school to learn the business of show business, with a goal of becoming an Entertainment Law specialist. I did an internship at the local District Attorney's Office and my whole career track changed its trajectory. Immediately, I saw that a criminal trial was like a little play—a story unfolding, with different points of view, heroes, villains, conflict, resolution—I was hooked! In law school, I complimented my theater training with courses in forensic oratory, public speaking, presentation skills, debate, and so on.

Now, of course, a criminal trial is *real* and not designed for entertainment, and the attorneys are not "acting" *per se*, but are presenting a point of view, the analogy of a courtroom with a theater, with the litigants as performers, and the audience as a jury, is a direct and startling parallel. Of course, there are differences, and any attorney who puts on a "show" is doomed to failure, but thinking of the trial process in the same way as creating a theater production will make it easier for the attorney who wants to win to persuade his "audience" in the most unusual device ever invented to resolve disputes and administer justice: a jury trial.

A jury is a group of random citizens — total strangers with absolutely no legal experience or knowledge of the matter to be decided — thrown together by Fate for the first time. This is your audience and it is your mission to persuade them — all of them, *unanimously*—that your side of the story is to be believed. This principle works for both the prosecutor and the defense attorney, or for the plaintiff's attorney and defense attorney in civil cases. Of course the facts of each case are the cards you are dealt, but knowing how to present the case, how to *tell the story*, is the skill which can often turn a losing hand into a winner, and, conversely, if you are tone deaf or unskilled in how you present your case, you can ruin your chances of success even if you began with all the advantage.

Prosecutors have a special task: to gain a conviction, they must persuade a jury to reach a unanimous verdict, meaning all 12 people must agree unanimously that someone committed a crime *beyond a reasonable doubt*. While the definition of "beyond a reasonable doubt" will differ from jurisdiction to jurisdiction, the general principle is that a jury must be convinced to a very high degree that a crime was committed, not just that it maybe was or even probably was, but that it was committed beyond a reasonable doubt and to a high level of certainty. If you step back and think about what a prosecutor is required to do, that's a pretty high hurdle. I had more than 100 jury trials in my 20 years as a prosecutor, and now, in retrospect, I have no idea how I won any of them!

Whether you are a prosecutor or a defense attorney, you never want to come across to your jury as theatrical. You don't want to be phony, or fake, or melodramatic. It can be a fine line, since you do always want to be interesting, logical, and emotionally invested in your case. Finding the right balance may take some years of practice and experience. You *do* want to look the jury in the eyes, and as honestly and openly as you can, convince them that you are right. You must persuade them that your position is legitimate, virtuous, and correct. That it will advance the cause of justice.

As the prosecutor, your "story" is usually told from the point of view of a victim or an investigating police officer. They say that some wrong has been committed. Someone was hurt or victimized. And here is the proof, this is the evidence. The evidence will be presented through testimony (more storytelling) and the presentation of demonstrative evidence. The testimony unfolds as several points of view from people with knowledge of the case, either first-hand personal knowledge ("I saw that man hit him!"), circumstantial knowledge through logical inferences ("I saw a footprint in the snow, so someone walked there."), and even through the testimony of expert witnesses ("I did a forensic analysis of the defendant's DNA."). This testimony is presented as a dialogue, through questions and answers, as the attorney and the witness go back and forth until the necessary and relevant information is described in court. But the attorney has at least two prescribed opportunities for a monologue: Opening Statement and Closing Argument. Being skilled in both formats—dialogue and monologue—can frequently make the difference, since it's not just *what* is said, but *how* it is said that can persuade the jury and determine the outcome.

When prosecutors present their case, it is their burden to move the case forward. But when clients come to see me now in my role as a defense attorney, they want *their side* of the story told, and they want their interests represented to the fullest possible extent. If the defendant's story or position can't be communicated effectively, he or she runs the risk of being convicted of a crime—with devastating personal consequences including potential incarceration and loss of freedom. The risk cannot be overstated. As a prosecutor, I took great satisfaction in helping victims of crimes. I prosecuted many homicides, child abuse cases and sexual assaults. These are cases with extremely tragic stories, with real life characters who had suffered greatly.

As a defense attorney, I help people just as much but in a different way. Either they actually have committed a crime and there is some reason which explains it, or they haven't committed a crime and the allegations are false or exaggerated. Sometimes they are overcharged, facing crimes which are beyond their level of guilt. Sometimes there are mitigating factors, such as mental illness, addiction issues, unbridled passion—something *human* which underlies what happened. Finding what caused the episode to happen, understanding the human motivations involved and developing a theme for your case are all essential components of a successful defense. But again, developing the craft of the presentation, the storytelling skills of an actor, learning that how to present the case is as important as knowing the facts of your case often makes the difference between a verdict of guilty or not guilty and between prison or freedom. My young son is amazed, "Dad! People *pay you money* to get up and just speak!" I always respond, "Yes, that's true, but I also have to think of clever things to say." It's a combination of what you say and how you say it.

You can be the world's most intelligent lawyer—book smart, library smart—but if you can't interpret your client's point of view and express it in the best light to your "audience" (Your audience can be a judge alone, a group of arbiters, or a jury; they are all decision-makers.), then it doesn't matter how smart you are. The art of communication is really the gift all great trial lawyers possess.

The gifted persuaders are not trying to con an audience or take on the role of a salesman. The courtroom litigators who shine are those who are advocates for a cause which he or she truly believes is right. It's an impromptu performance from the heart with a mix of compassion and logic while remaining ethical, honest, and credible. Your audience must believe you, and unless you believe it yourself, they never will. I once had a juror tell me, "I had no idea what the case was about, but you seemed so sure of yourself, I just decided to vote for your side."

STAGE LEFT, STAGE RIGHT, FRONT AND CENTER

These are the three components of classic Greek forensic oratory: logos (or logic), ethos (your ethics or credibility), and pathos (your emotions). These are intertwined dramatic concepts that have been analyzed and studied since the days of Greek theater, and they are still critical to an understanding of how to effectively present a legal argument. Analysts now know that an effective speaker will weave each of these concepts into his presentation, so that listeners will bond with the speaker. If you're logical, have energy, emotion, and conviction, people will be persuaded to trust you and then they will believe you. People in general (and jurors in particular) will say, "Yes, I agree with this lawyer. I believe him/her. I believe that defendant did/didn't do that. I find him guilty/not guilty." The same concepts hold true for sentencing hearings in front of the judge: your presentation must try to convince the judge to give your client a break, not to send him or her to jail, to show mercy and see what the underlying reasons are which lead to this unfortunate conclusion.

Every case and every defendant has a story. There is an endless variety of stories: usually tragedies, there aren't a lot of comedies in the courtroom. As an attorney, you must gain an understanding of what emotions to evoke in grabbing the attention of the audience, because only then can you persuade them to adopt your point of view. But to win, your client's story must be effectively communicated.

Though I don't see my television years on soap operas as greatly helpful in illustrating these concepts, I don't run from my theatrical background as a professional actor either. It's just who I am. To the extent it can help someone, I will utilize the skills gained from the stage and adopt them to help the victims I fought for as a prosecutor and for my clients now that I am a defense attorney. I hope it helps my clients, and indirectly, it also helps me. Eventually you gain a reputation. Ideally, people in your community say, "You want to go and see Alex Foster because he really knows how to command the courtroom. He has a lot of presence. You need a good lawyer who can do that."

Once learned, a background in the theater and the basic skills you acquire never really leave you once you get up in a courtroom. You don't lose them. Every time I get up to speak, I want to speak clearly so my listener can hear me. I want to use language that's appropriate to my listener. I can talk to a jury or a judge, or any type of witness which may come along. I've cross examined murderers and rapists. I've called generals and nuns to the witness stand. Humanity is extremely diverse. You've got to be able to communicate with everyone. For years, I prosecuted child abuse cases with very young victims. I once qualified a 5-year-old to testify in court. Using the skills of an actor allows you to adopt a flexibility so that you can talk to anyone in the context of a trial, on the stage of the courtroom. I want to look each person in the eye. I want to make sure that my voice is clear and compelling. I focus on gesturing and moving appropriately. Like props, I present exhibits, papers, and documents in a clear way. All of these elements are woven together and presented as a little play— a performance, a tragedy—but with real-life consequences.

But the attorney is not just acting in someone else's script. In a criminal trial, the attorney is the author, the playwright, the director, the producer, and the star. You take on all of those roles and, ultimately, your job is to help somebody. It's not entertainment. You're not there to make people laugh or experience something for their enlightenment or education. As a defense attorney, you're there to protect someone, to represent that person, because if you don't, he or she might go to jail or worse. If you're trying to defend a death penalty case, you may literally have your client's life at stake. That might be melodramatic, but try to imagine someone you love is facing such a terrible risk, the pressure and stress is inestimable. So, everything you can use to help advance your client's cause—every fair, ethical tactic you can employ and every skill you can learn about how to present the story—is invaluable.

In the courtroom, you and the judge and jury are all playing out a story with what actors and playwrights call "point of view." Point of view is simply how someone sees or remembers something. It is very common that the exact same episode will be perceived totally differently, even from people who both experienced it. As humans, we instinctively know this. We experience it daily in our normal lives. Human memory is faulty. People are motivated to exaggerate. People lie. It happens in virtually every criminal trial. So, often a trial is like three different stories: the protagonist's story, the antagonist's story, and the truth which is usually somewhere in the middle. There is a rise, a fall, a denouement, a hero, and an anti-hero. As every criminal trial in a courtroom is a story, attorneys can benefit from understanding the common elements and structure of classic storytelling. It's really all the same. The play's the thing.

Every play by Shakespeare has five acts. The plays always follow a similar structure or architecture: a beginning, a middle, and an end. All types of stories, including a criminal trial, should follow this same classic structure. The hero-villain dynamic has been ingrained in us by our culture; every time we watch a TV show or movie, every book that we read, every story that we hear has this basic counterbalance of protagonist against antagonist, the hero versus the villain. In the courtroom, of course, each side tries to identify these roles so they fit into their theory of the case. As the defense attorney, who is your hero? It is the defendant. When you are a prosecutor, your hero is either the police detective or maybe the victim. Who is your villain?

Obviously, in the prosecutor's version of the play, the defendant plays that part. A defense attorney's job is to challenge that and offer a different theory.

Human beings have been telling stories since we were cavemen around the campfire talking about the buffalo hunt or escaping from the big bear. It's an ancient human art form as old as dance or music. It's communication. It's language. It's as primitive as humanity itself. The ability to tell a good story—to use imagination, language, and sense of drama to evoke images in the imaginations of others, the ability to *persuade* it's just in our DNA. Each of us has the capacity to bring it out. In the courtroom, when it's all boiled down, it's the same thing: tell the story.

A great lawyer can take a losing hand and win because he's a great communicator and he's convincing. If you're inadequate or don't understand the principles of effective storytelling, you can have all the cards and still lose.

Students can learn these concepts in law school. That's why we do mock trials. There, you are given a hypothetical case file with witnesses and evidence. Usually, these case files are very balanced and give each side something to work with. One day you argue one side, and the next day, you argue the other side of the same story. Sometimes you win as a prosecutor on Tuesday. When the script is flipped, you win on Wednesday as a defense attorney. Why? The facts are exactly the same. It tests the students' ability to tell the story, and how you present your case often determines which side prevails. Because all litigators are naturally very competitive, it is axiomatic that all prosecutors and defense attorneys want to win. Devoting attention to how the story is told can make the difference between a victory and a devastating defeat. After all, the play's the thing.

THE COURTROOM LEARNING CURVE

So, let's say you've made it through those three tough years of law school. You took your Bar Exam preparation course and survived the Bar Exam. A month or two later, the letter came which had "Congratulations!" as the first word in the first sentence. You passed. You'll be sworn in as an actual attorney soon. You can hardly believe it. Now what? Well, if you want to learn how to become a great litigator, I'd suggest researching all of the local prosecutors' offices and Public Defenders' offices in all of the jurisdictions around you. Because there is no doubt: a novice prosecutor or public defender will learn how to survive and flourish inside a courtroom faster than any other way. I promise. Just as you can't learn how to swim or get a black belt in karate from a book, you have to just do it to learn how to do it.

As a prosecutor or public defender, you learn how the complex game of a courtroom trial is played. For almost everyone, the courtroom is alien territory, it's like a foreign country. The language is different, with obscure Latin phrases. The procedures and customs are different. The rules of engagement are unfamiliar. For example, when a lawyer asks questions, the defendants or the witnesses must answer them. They're not allowed to ask questions back. This is all very different from the normal rules of conversation which you've adopted over the course of your whole life. It's not like those family free-for-all arguments at Thanksgiving where you can interrupt each other. You can shout. You can accuse people. You can divert them by going on to another topic. It doesn't work that way in the courtroom. But, once you master the courtroom rules of engagement, you have an enormous advantage over your witness, since you know the rules and they don't.

The courtroom is a very orderly, controlled environment with a judge who enforces the decorum of the courtroom. He or she rules on questions, sustains objections, or overrules them. It's a very foreign environment for most people since virtually all of the witnesses will be unfamiliar with this dynamic. The actual terms used when posing valid objections are totally new phrases and concepts for the typical layperson: improper foundation, hearsay, assuming facts not in evidence, leading, compound questions! These complex rules need to be learned through repetition and experience; there is simply no other way. That takes time. Since prosecutors and public defenders are in court all the time, they learn these skills rapidly. I tell young people, "If you want to be a great courtroom lawyer, either become a young prosecutor or a young public defender because then you have to be in court every day."

When I first started in the 1980s, I was in court every single day five days a week, and I had about 50 cases in misdemeanor court each docket. Do the numbers: you literally have hundreds of cases a month and thousands each year. I used to keep a running tally or diary of my Bench trials (misdemeanor trials before a judge only, not a jury). Before I got promoted to the higher-level felony court with cases in front of juries, I had tried more than 300 bench trials. There is just no other way to get that type of hands-on experience in a corporate law firm where first-year associates spend 60 hours or more a week in the research library and never even see a courtroom up close.

So what actually happens in each of those 300 little cases? Well, a police officer or a complaining citizen, will say that something happened which wasn't legal. Somebody stole something. Somebody punched somebody. Someone was drunk. Someone was smoking marijuana. Someone took advantage of someone.

Or an infinite variety of scenarios where someone did something society has judged to be immoral, unfair, or just anti-social. As you prosecute hundreds of these disputes, you learn the rules very quickly. You make mistakes, and you learn not to repeat them. You gain confidence talking in front of a crowded courtroom. You learn organizational skills. You become a trial attorney. The learning curve is not curved, it's nearly vertical because you're learning so fast. Remember that friend of yours in law school who took that big-paying job as an associate in the litigation department of a private law firm? He or she is making money but not learning how to be a trial attorney. I've known those associates; some of them *never* go to court. Not even once.

Yes, in the beginning, you may be awkward and miss important things. There is the potential to be embarrassed, to fail. No one likes to lose, and trial attorneys are notoriously competitive and egocentric. You are very exposed standing up there, and it's so easy for people who don't really have the courage to do this type of work to be critical. The risks are obvious, and this isn't a game, it's real with real people's lives being affected. But it is also just . . . thrilling! If you have the strength of personality to fight through the tough times, the rewards are inestimable. When you directly right a wrong, when you help a vulnerable victim achieve justice, when you protect the community, all of the stresses of learning seem insignificant. And, the learning curve goes straight up, so if you adopt a boot camp mentality, meaning that this initial phase of your career passes quickly, you just have to fight your way through it. Because, over time, you start to put together how the rules work. Through experience, you learn which questions are effective and how to control witnesses when you cross examine them. You learn how to do opening statements and closing arguments, and make objections. You learn the rules of evidence, and you see case law and precedent convinces the judge. You learn the "elements" of the various crimes and you begin to assimilate the standard Jury Instructions as you hear the judge charge the jury. Over time, these things start to correlate and repeat themselves. Formulas emerge. And you begin to tell yourself, "I've had a case like this one before." Soon, you have something which can only be attained one way: you have *experience*.

For example, many District Attorney's offices start their beginning prosecutors in Traffic Court. It is often a launching pad for brand-new prosecutors, because you literally do hundreds of drunk driving cases. After a month or two, you begin to realize that all of these cases are pretty much the same. Someone drove a car, and then they did something that drew the attention of the police such as speeding or crashing or swerving. So, a police officer pulled the car over, and observed something that made him or her think that the driver was drunk. The police officer put the driver through some tests of coordination or split attention on the roadside. The driver did or did not take a breathalyzer which resulted in a specific number reflecting the amount of alcohol in the blood stream. Almost every case falls into a formula or pattern like this, so, with repetition, you start to see these similarities, and you start to gain confidence. You've seen this before. You can do this. You become an expert yourself. You find yourself winning regularly. And then you start applying this learning mode to the other types of misdemeanors: all shoplifting, all fistfights, all possession of marijuana cases follow their own patterns.

Then, once all these arcane rules and formulas become less foreign, you feel as if you've finally learned how to play the game. But you've learned more than just technical skills, you are also contemporaneously learning how to assess people. You hear so much dishonesty from witnesses, you learn how to be a human lie detector. Social skills and psychology play a part. This is a people business. If it were not, we'd just type information into a computer and the computer would analyze the facts and say, "The defendant is guilty," or, "The defendant is not guilty; the case hasn't been proven," or, "The evidence is insufficient." In this people business, how you communicate and persuade somebody is what makes the difference in these results. As the prosecutor, you definitely want to hear the word "Guilty" a lot; as the defense attorney, you relish those dramatic "Not Guilty" verdicts with a huge swell of personal pride.

WHEN THE WHITE HAT TURNS BLACK

It's been frequently said that the prosecutor wears a white hat. You are the champion of justice. You ride in and save the day, you're the Sheriff in the town facing down outlaws at high noon. People in the courthouse community respect you. You get to know the strengths and weaknesses of the judges, opponents, clerks, bailiffs, police officers, and all of the other people in the system. So, when you make the transition from a prosecutor to a defense attorney, to the extent that you have interacted successfully with these people, it is likely that all of that goodwill comes with you.

That transition works for another reason. When the players know you, they give you the benefit of the doubt. They know you are not dishonest. You're not just someone who represents rapists and murderers for the big bucks—a mercenary. Instead, you're seen as a former prosecutor who used to put the bad guys in jail. Now, you're helping people in a different, more direct way, you're defending them, protecting their rights. You're bringing your credibility across the courtroom to the other side. The judges that admired your work or thought that you were fighting a good fight all those years as a prosecutor know that you're the same person with the same presence. By then, you'll know so many police officers. You can go out in the courtroom hallway and say, "Hey Billy, I represent this kid. What's the deal?" They will in all likelihood talk to you. You can say, "Let's give this kid a break. It's his first time. He's sorry. He'll pay back the money for the window he broke." They'll say, "That's okay with me, sounds fair." You can ask the officer to go tell the young prosecutor to wrap this one up. You can resolve things because people know you and trust you. That's a *huge* advantage in transitioning from a prosecutor to a defense attorney.

In my jurisdiction, I know the prosecutors; some of whom are still in the State's Attorney's Office after 25 to 30 years. I left after 20 years. I've been a lawyer for almost 30 years. There are prosecutors I now have cases against who came to my wedding. We socialize. Our children have played together. We have played softball together. It helps enormously to have relationships with people on the other side of the courtroom, because I can easily approach a senior prosecutor now and say something like, "Listen, Robert, can you help me out? I know this woman stole a lot of money from her company, but she needed it to pay for her mother's medical bills. She can pay it all back. Can we do a misdemeanor plea with no jail? This isn't a case where the State needs a conviction for a felony with the possibility of three years of incarceration." So, if you play your cards right, you do get preferential treatment in a way, because friendship makes the communication between the adversaries a lot easier. There is less friction and a better chance at cooperation. This gives your client an enormous advantage.

I work almost exclusively in the one county where I was a prosecutor, but I've traveled around the state of Maryland and appeared in many counties. It's abundantly clear to me that when

I travel, the courtroom personnel—the prosecutors, judges, and others in the system—respect my ability to play the game, but they don't know me personally. There's a certain level of thinking: "You're a stranger and you don't get the home cooking."

In the jurisdiction where I practice, I know every single one of the 60+ prosecutors. Sure, I argue or clash with some of them, but I would count most of them as personal friends. It's the same with the judges. Judges are generally senior lawyers, elected from the top prosecutors and the top defense attorneys. I know many of the judges as personal friends. Of course, you shouldn't attempt to use that to your advantage in an obvious or blatant way, but the fact of the matter is, when you walk into the courtroom and somebody that you've known for 25–30 years is sitting on the bench, of course it can be helpful. They know you, but they also know you will play your role, just as they will play theirs.

The courtroom is like a stage, after all. We each play our parts. But, underneath the role playing, they *know* you and they trust you. They know you're not going to lie to them. They know you're just doing your job, but you're doing it fairly and honorably and ethically. And if they rule against you, they know that you will understand it's their job, too. We each play our roles and we move through the process. Because, as I've said, the play's the thing!

WEARING THE BLACK HAT WITH PRIDE AND STYLE

In many ways, a defense attorney is like a surgeon doing a heart transplant. It requires a tremendous amount of experience, skill, education, and focus—and effort! If you botch this, you could be changing the course of your client's life forever. In my own particular career path, making the transition to defense attorney from prosecutor took me 20 years. Most defense attorneys who were former prosecutors only wore the white hat for a few years until they nailed down the basics and got a sense of how it all works. Many prosecutors leave after two or three years because the financial benefits of private practice lure them away. They are often at a time in their lives where either student loans beckon, or they desire to get married and start a family and harsh economics influence the switch.

Attorneys specialize in the law just like doctors specialize in body parts or systems. Nobody would go to a podiatrist or a psychiatrist to do a heart transplant. They would go to a cardiologist. When someone goes to law school, he or she can major in different things. Some people are interested in corporate law or real estate law; some people are interested in the philosophy of Constitutional issues.

For those who specialize in criminal justice, the emphasis in law school focuses on "Criminal Law," "Criminal Procedure," and "Evidence." Along with a sense of the history of Anglo-American jurisprudence and the evolution of "Constitutional Law," those are really the three areas to master for a person who wants to become proficient in a courtroom practicing criminal law. It goes far beyond just knowing the difference between the various crimes. Understanding the legal distinctions between murder and manslaughter, between first-degree murder and second-degree murder, is just the beginning.

"Criminal Procedure" is the law school class which teaches the set of rules governing the way that a trial plays out. It is necessary to learn the procedures for a grand jury, an indictment, a preliminary hearing, an arraignment, a plea, a trial, and so forth. Lastly, a criminal lawyer needs to perfect his handling of the rules of "Evidence." What are proper courtroom questions for both direct testimony and cross-examination? What is inadmissible hearsay? What constitutes a proper foundation, etc.? There are required rules and methods for introducing exhibits, documents, photographs, and all of the myriad ways to move around a courtroom and conduct business properly. Once an attorney gets a feel for those three things, he can go into a courtroom and represent somebody.

As an accused person, how do you find a good criminal defense attorney? First of all, you need to look at a specialist who has specific experience in the types of issues involved in your unique case. This distinction goes beyond knowing basic criminal law versus being an attorney who can complete the paperwork necessary to close the deal when you buy a house. Really good DUI lawyers, for example, spends lots of time learning the minutia of the technical and scientific methods for collection of breath and blood samples. They know what ampoules are, they speak the language of "BAC." They know what things like the horizontal gaze nystagmus test is. A DUI specialist probably spends much less time on understanding the pathology of the mind of an arsonist, the psychological proclivities of a child sexual predator, how ballistics comparisons work, or what mitochondrial DNA is, and on and on and on.

A lot of lawyers throw a shingle on a door and say, "I'm good at divorces, personal injury cases, wills, trusts and estates, and criminal law." That's analogous to a general practitioner physician saying, "I'm a psychologist, a foot doctor, a cancer specialist, and I also pull teeth." It's impossible to be good at everything. Find a lawyer who has a specific background in the kind of defense that you need. Go on the Internet and search websites; you'll see people that specialize in every imaginable type of case.

Second, you need to search for a former prosecutor or public defender. I get calls every now and then from people who need help outside my geographic jurisdiction. The conversation might go something like this:

> *Caller:* "My son got caught drunk driving at his college in South Carolina. We need help!"

> *Alex:* "Well, I think South Carolina is a great place. I love Charleston. But, to be direct, I don't know anything about South Carolina law and I can't practice there. I only have a Bar license in the State of Maryland."

> *Caller:* "How do I find a good lawyer in South Carolina?"

> *Alex:* "I'd suggest getting online and look at attorney websites. Look for a former prosecutor or a former public defender in the county where your kid's crime took place. These attorneys will know the judges and the local rules. They will have tremendous local courtroom experience because they learned the ropes right in that courthouse. I might have a lot more experience, but I will be viewed as a stranger. You're always much better off finding someone with local experience."

Other factors come into play when you're looking for an attorney and affordability can sometimes be a determining factor. Lawyers are very expensive. I often tell my drunk driving clients that the worst part of the whole experience is the total financial cost. That bottle of wine you consumed can turn out to be extremely expensive.

Let's say that you qualify for a public defender. The Supreme Court ruled in 1963 (*Gideon v Wainwright*) that all indigent or poor defendants are legally *entitled* to a free lawyer. The Justices said that it's simply not fair to have a poor person, a homeless person, or an uneducated person walk into a courtroom alone to face a prosecutor and a judge. It was just inequitable. Since fairness or equity is the goal we strive for in our jurisprudence, that ruling founded the concept of the public defender.

So, because most middle-class or working class people won't qualify for a public defender, they sometimes are faced with a cruel dilemma: representing themselves or hiring a private attorney. An old and tired (but true) adage says, "Anyone who represents himself has a fool for a client." When people call me and say, "Why can't I just represent myself?" I use different analogies to convey what a terrible idea that is. I might advise: "Well, if you had an abscessed tooth, would you pull it out yourself? You could just go to the garage and get a pair of pliers and you could probably pull out your own tooth. But I wouldn't recommend that. You may actually do more damage. You may cause nerve damage. You may end up going to an oral surgeon who will cost you thousands and thousands of dollars, when a simple, proper removal of the tooth would end up costing you much less." Don't ever try to represent yourself in a courtroom.

THE CHIPS ARE STACKED VERY HIGH

Going to court is very serious business. What happens there can literally change your life. As a poker player might say, "All in!" The chips are stacked very high when you are a criminal defendant. An attorney can guide you, advise you, and defend you. Sometimes people represent themselves on very small misdemeanors or civil infractions like jaywalking, carrying a beer in public, etc. They generally end up getting sentenced with community service or the case is dismissed from court altogether. So, probably even with an attorney, the result would be the same no matter what. But, beyond that very low level of courtroom appearance, you should never attempt to represent yourself.

One of the biggest risks in not having a case handled properly is to have a permanent criminal record. The job market is incredibly tight. The economy is tough. Launching a new career is highly competitive. Employers regularly conduct background checks. In most places, anybody can look at your background online. The last thing you want on your permanent, public record is a conviction, particularly for any crime that might call your honesty into question. Employers don't want to hire anyone who has a history of any kind of criminal behavior, especially involving drugs or alcohol. Even worse, if your record reflects issues around honesty or violent crimes, you're in trouble. If you've been convicted of something like domestic violence or hurting a child, your chances of surviving a job interview process go exponentially down even further. However, the good news is that most jurisdictions have legal provisions which can remove a conviction for first time offenses. So, hiring an attorney who will know how to erase a conviction from your record is worth the investment many times over.

One misstep as a youth can derail or haunt a young person for many, many years unless it's taken care of correctly at the beginning. A small price to pay now, considering the hundreds of thousands of dollars earned during a long career. Imagine if that 20-year-old who got caught smoking marijuana didn't get into medical school years later? Or when applying for law school, your son has to check the box indicating a criminal conviction because of a drunk driving conviction at the beach when he was on Spring Break? The importance of keeping a clean record cannot be overstated; a future job could be at risk, entrance into that post-graduate business school, or a house loan from the bank. And in this Google age, anyone can do a quick internet search and discover someone's personal history. Court records are generally public records unless an attorney takes steps to shield them or otherwise get them erased. It's best to have an experienced attorney protect your future. Forever is a very long time.

GUILT, INNOCENCE AND REASONABLE DOUBT: WHAT DOES IT ALL MEAN?

Obviously, while a vast majority of cases are resolved by way of a plea agreement, there are always puzzles which cannot be solved; knots which cannot be untied. In the criminal law, we call these stalemates jury trials. If a case has overwhelming evidence, it's usually a plea. However, in case where the State's evidence is faulty or weak or fragmented, a defendant might weigh his or her odds and roll the dice. And, of course, even cynics will admit that there actually are innocent people wrongfully charged with a crime (although from my experience over the last 25+ years, this is an exceedingly rare event).

Remember, the jury doesn't have to find that you're innocent. The jury has to find that the State failed to prove their case beyond a reasonable doubt. It is a whole different concept. In England, they have three choices: guilty, not guilty, and not proven. Do most "not guilty" cases in America fall into that middle category? They're not proven. It doesn't mean that the defendant didn't commit the act which constitutes a crime, but that the prosecution simply didn't have the evidence. Unproved is not innocent. In America, we call that "not guilty."

Last summer, I represented a young man in a very serious First Degree Rape case. My client protested vehemently that he was not guilty, "I didn't rape that girl!" he said over and over. I'm usually suspicious in situations where my own client claims his or her innocence so passionately. However, once we got the discovery, nothing the "victim" said seemed to make sense with the physical evidence. We hired a private investigator to get photos from an ATM, to track down her cell phone records, to review the hospital records, and the case started disintegrating before our eyes. This young man was locked up in jail pretrial on a very high bond and it turned out that the young woman complainant was *completely* making up the accusation that she was raped. She went so far as to cut herself, go to the hospital, and say that my client raped her at knifepoint. Fortunately, we were able to show that her allegations were completely fabricated. I'll never forget the accused, my client, protesting to me, "I'm   not pleading guilty to *anything*. I did *not* rape that girl." And the prosecutor was determined to keep moving forward. We were on a dangerous collision course towards a trial until I was able to convince the prosecutor to drop the charges. So, all's well that ends well. But, I will never forget the unfairness of it all. First Degree Rape carries a potential prison sentence of *Life*. Talk about high drama? No wonder the courtroom has been compared to a stage by many.

American history is replete with false and unjust convictions. Juries are very fickle. They like to convict people. They also look at the type of crime committed. Certain crimes are so shocking (child abuse, pedophilia, animal cruelty) that the presumption of innocence is often negated simply by the horrific nature of the charges. Average people aren't accustomed to hearing or even thinking about such repugnant things. There is an old saying that it's better to let a guilty man go free rather than to convict an innocent man. Yet, these things happen every day in our courts, guilty people beat the charges and walk free, and sometimes (but not often) completely innocent people are railroaded. No one said this system was perfect.

Many people get frustrated by the notion that a guilty person would walk free because a jury was fooled or incompetent. Of course, all the defense attorney has to do is find one or two jurors who have a "reasonable doubt." Attorneys shoot for a "hung jury," meaning a jury which is split, undecided and not unanimous. To achieve that, a skilled defense attorney just needs a couple of jurors to say, "I just don't know. I just don't think I can convict." They have not reached unanimity. Remember, 12 to 0 is not an easy task for a prosecutor. If the verdict is 11 to 1, the prosecution hasn't convicted the defendant. Anything less than a unanimous verdict goes in favor of the defense. If that happens, the State can elect to retry the case again, but, in my experience, the usual result is a very favorable plea offer to the defendant. Prosecutors hate to retry cases. Witnesses abhor coming back. Vulnerable victims, like rape victims or children, don't want to go through the trauma of testifying all over again. So, mistrials/hung juries usually work out in the defendant's benefit.

Defense attorneys know that sometimes their clients will go off to prison. It's just a harsh reality of the job. It's just an occupational hazard. I once saw a 20-year old defendant I represented plead guilty to Second Degree Murder and get sentenced to 30 years in prison. Sounds like a disaster. But, he was charged with First Degree Murder which carries a Life sentence and the State's case was very strong. So, is that a victory or a defeat? It's just so hard to say, it's all relative. Most prosecutors don't keep statistics. I think the general public wants to know, "What's your winning percentage?" But, it's not like computing a batting average in baseball. A prosecutor could win 100% of the cases if he took only easy ones. A really top prosecutor might win only 50% of his cases if he was trying the really difficult ones, like child abuse cases or sexual assaults. So, who's really the better prosecutor? Defense attorneys can't categorize cases neatly either; they have to define a "win" differently. Since full acquittals are extremely rare, victory comes in other disguises, such as limiting the amount of jail time to something reasonably brief or having a major felony reduced to a simple misdemeanor.

THE CURTAIN BEGINS TO FALL

Our criminal justice system is often criticized. The history of man has shown us a variety of social systems designed by people to keep order. It seems to be a universal truth that all people desire justice for wrongs committed against them. This emotion, "justice," is as ingrained in the human psyche as much as any other base emotion, as deeply rooted as "revenge", "mercy", or Biblical concepts such as "an eye for an eye."

However, our current jury system can be directly traced to the concepts of dispute resolution as promulgated in the Magna Carta. Our modern rules for weighing evidence, for hearing testimony from witnesses, and especially for the participation by peers as jurors evolved from concepts of justice first decreed by King John of England. Over time, these concepts developed into what we now know as the trial by jury. Before that, the King as absolute divine Ruler decided everything like a tyrant. Simple peasants and craftsmen found that they at least had a fighting chance in front of jury of their neighbors and townsmen. It sure beat the King deciding. So, while the jury system has evolved over the centuries, the concept of peer judgment remains intact.

And, while our present courtroom advocacy system is very far from perfect, it certainly is the best design created by man to orderly arbitrate issues of law, justice, and fairness.

There are certainly many exceptions to this rule, some of which I've recited myself here in this chapter, but despite that, I truly believe that our criminal justice system is the best we faulty humans could ever devise. Of course, there are miscarriages of justice from time to time, but generally, I think this system does an exceptionally accurate job of finding the truth. There are many places in the world where freedom is virtually non-existent. In those places, there is no such thing as free speech or a courtroom system that provides equal rights to both sides. Yes, our jury system is very flawed. Guilty people go free and innocent people are occasionally convicted. There has been—and there still is—racial prejudice, gender inequality, and deprivation of equity for many. There is occasional injustice. Having said that, I still believe it's the best criminal justice system in the world for resolving issues. I know of no other method for finding the truth and achieving justice that is better.

(This content should be used for informational purposes only. It does not create an attorney-client relationship with any reader and should not be construed as legal advice. If you need legal advice, please contact an attorney in your community who can assess the specifics of your situation.)

6

<hr>

A Lawyers Job Is To Protect Your Client's Constitutional Rights Regardless Of His Guilt Or Innocence

by Lorin J. Zaner, Esq.

Lorin J. Zaner, Esq.
Law Office of Lorin J. Zaner
Toledo, Ohio
www.ohiocriminaldefenselawyer.com

Criminal defense attorney Lorin J. Zaner achieved his Bachelor of Arts degree in Chemical Engineering from the University of Toledo where he graduated cum laude in 1970. Zaner earned his Juris Doctorate from the same university five years later.

Attorney Zaner makes his home and his office in Toledo, Ohio where he practices criminal and juvenile law. While he does not limit his criminal practice in any significant way, his expertise is in the defense against allegations of civil and criminal child abuse as well as shaken baby cases. His background in science has proven to be beneficial in those cases where forensic evidence plays an important role. Zaner has a continuing commitment to staying abreast of the science around false accusations of child abuse, which can be the most difficult to defend. Zaner is admitted to the bar and may practice in Ohio, Michigan, and in Federal Court.

A Lawyers Job Is To Protect Your Client's Constitutional Rights Regardless Of His Guilt Or Innocence

Early in my career, I worked as a public defender in a Juvenile Court, but now I am a criminal and juvenile defense attorney. I practice in both Ohio and Michigan. Some tell me I am something of an expert in matters involving child abuse charges and shaken baby syndrome. I have a much broader practice, but I do spend a good bit of my time defending people who are accused of harming children. My mother wondered how I could represent people who have been charged with such heinous crimes. She came to court with me one day and watched what was happening to a family with someone who was being falsely accused. After that, she finally understood why I chose this area of law.

People sometimes grapple with the concept of defending a person who may be guilty of a terrible crime. In my opinion, it is ten times harder to represent an innocent person than it is a guilty person. I do not like to lose and I work just as hard in either situation, but you have everything to lose when someone is innocent. You do not have nearly as much to lose when representing someone who is clearly guilty. The bottom line is that if you cannot represent someone because you know that person is guilty, then you need to get out of this business. Everyone is innocent until he or she is proven guilty. Everybody has a constitutional right to defend himself. Everybody has a right to have a competent lawyer and the lawyer should do everything in his power to protect his client's rights.

During my juvenile public defender days, I often questioned the judge about how the law and justice meshes, which is not always clear in emotional cases like the ones I saw in court. The judge would always tell me, "You're here to help children. You're here to look out for their best interests." The judge was wrong.

Your job as a lawyer is to protect your client's constitutional rights regardless of his guilt or innocence. If there is a motion to suppress or if there are objections that need to be made at trial, you have an ethical obligation to do all of those things. The best interest of the child does not come into play until and unless your client is found guilty of the charges. You have to protect your client's constitutional rights because those constitutional rights are the very foundation of our entire justice system. If each person is not defended with the belief he is innocent until proven guilty, the whole system breaks down. Lawyers are here to protect their clients and to keep the system operating as it was meant to do when it was created. For me, and for most other attorneys, I would rather have 100 guilty people walk in the street than one innocent person in custody.

ALLEGATIONS OF MOLESTATION

Many times, molestation allegations occur in custody battles and divorce battles. It is the best way for the person who is making the allegations to gain a major advantage in the custody battle. The most important thing that a person facing such allegations has to do is to hire an attorney who is skilled in this area of law. A lawyer might say he specializes or is very capable, but he may not have sufficient experience or expertise in these cases. Handling charges such as these is a completely different ball game than handling a burglary or assault. The dynamics are different and how you strategize and implement your defense in these cases are worlds apart from most criminal matters.

When searching for an attorney, do not just look at a website to get your information. Interview the attorney—ask questions as if you were hiring him for a job, because you are. When you are interviewing the lawyer, some of the things you should ask include how many cases he has handled, how many cases he has actually taken to trial and what were the results of those trials. Ask the lawyer for the names of some of those cases so you can look them up to verify the results because many lawyers will say they can handle these types of cases and they really haven't.

This is very important: If someone comes to your door, such as the police or Protective Services, and they want to talk to you about allegations, you can only hurt yourself by talking to them. You cannot help yourself if you talk to them without a lawyer. The law states that you must specifically ask for a lawyer. You cannot say, "Should I get a lawyer? Do you think I should get a lawyer?" That's not good enough. You must specifically say, *"I want to speak with a lawyer."* I had a client who was charged with 15 counts of rape involving two stepchildren. If convicted, he would go to prison for life. After he was found not guilty, he got me a t-shirt that says, "You have the right to remain silent. Anything you say can and will be misinterpreted and used against you." That is exactly how it is.

When these allegations are made, the police and protective services do not do a good job of investigating. When a child says, "This has happened," they take it as gospel. At that point, they stop looking for all the surrounding circumstances and/or all the reasons why these allegations are being made. You cannot help yourself by talking to the police without a lawyer.

Many lawyers take the position, "Never talk to the police." That is also a mistake and the one who says this is someone who does not understand the dynamics of how to handle child abuse cases. There are times when you do want to talk to the police but, once again, only with a lawyer who understands and knows what he is doing. I have had situations where I represented professors and other professionals where, if anything hit the press, their lives and careers would be instantly over—their lives would be ruined. They cannot continue to do what they do under allegations like these. Therefore, there may be times when you want to talk to police or Protective Services but only when you have an attorney there with you.

Many lawyers who are being considered to represent someone accused of this kind of thing believe, "Well, I'm an excellent trial lawyer. I can cross-examine well and I will get the child to tell the truth based on my skills at cross-examining." That lawyer is not prepared or sufficiently educated to represent anyone in such a case. He does not understand the dynamics of this area of law and is not aware of the psychological research that has been completed in this area so you need to keep looking for the right attorney. You see, you do not try the case based on what the child says at the time of trial. You really need to focus on what led up to these allegations. Was the child in trouble looking for a way to get out? Was a parent upset for some reason and looking to make an accusation against the father? (Normally it is the father who is charged in these cases, but I have had cases where mothers have been charged.) Therefore, you need to look at all the dynamics to see what is going on and why this is happening.

You also need to know if you can avoid the charges being filed. Sometimes they will offer polygraphs. In most states, polygraphs are not admissible under certain circumstances. Polygraphs are not perfect. You, as the accused, should discuss this with an attorney before you ever consider taking a polygraph. Be very careful before stipulating to the admissibility of the polygraph. Essentially, this would mean that if you pass the test, the polygraph results come into evidence. However, if you fail, it still comes into evidence. Make sure you understand the consequences before taking a stipulated polygraph.

If charges are filed, your lawyer needs to immediately begin doing numerous things on your behalf. Pre-trial motions need to be filed before trial. Investigations need to be done to find witnesses. Legal research needs to be completed. During the trial, numerous objections and other matters need to be made to make sure you have a record of your objections in case you lose. Obviously, the goal is not to lose but it is something you must consider.

The other thing that is important to understand is that, in order for these cases to be handled properly, a great deal of money is involved. These cases are very expensive, but remember, the rest of your life is at stake. The interesting thing is, when it comes to money to be provided to a court-appointed attorney for the lawyer himself and for investigators and experts, the court only has to provide limited funds. The State does not have to provide the funds for the best expert. Many court-appointed attorneys are every bit as good as a private attorney is, but the difference is tied to the funding the court is willing to provide in order to defend the case. The prosecution, on the other hand, seems to have unlimited funding. They can bring in numerous experts at no cost. However, the defense is usually limited by their client's lack of funds and ability to come up with the resources necessary to adequately fight the case. Public defenders and clients with limited resources are at a huge disadvantage.

When you are in trial, it is obviously important that you cooperate with your attorney. Many issues must be taken into consideration during the trial. I have had a number of cases where I have had experts lined up to testify and have decided not to call them because I have been able to turn the state's experts, even police officers, into my own experts. Even when your client does have the funds, you have to let the lawyer try the case as he believes it needs to be tried.

Another key element is whether or not you allow your client to testify. If the defendant does not testify, the prosecutor cannot use cross-examination to confuse the defendant into saying something damaging on the stand. People become nervous and mess up when they are on the witness stand. This decision needs to be the lawyer's call. I am familiar with a case where the defendant took the stand and he was asked whether he molested the alleged victim. He hesitated for about a minute before he responded, "No." Obviously, he was found guilty. Many things must be considered before you make a determination as to whether a client should testify. I do not like to put clients on the stand but every case is different. Every case has to be analyzed differently as to how it is going to be tried. No two cases are alike. Obviously, no two defendants are alike.

During *voir dire*, the process of selecting a jury, when you are choosing the jury members, you can prepare the jury for the possibility that your client might not testify in his own defense, which is, of course, the defendant's right. By doing this advance preparation, the jury may not hold it against your client. In reality, the defendant has already testified. He said, "I didn't do it," when he entered a not guilty plea. The point here is that, at trial, things change and move rapidly with regard to the "pulse" of the case. It is a fluid situation and a good lawyer must be able to make decisions as things change so that the impact is positive. Furthermore, you need to set forth to the jury your philosophy as to what this case is about and why they are here in court. If you cannot come up with a motivation for why the allegations are being made, then your client is going to be in a lot of trouble.

I became involved in a case after the defendant was found guilty of a sexual offense. I filed a motion for a new trial. At trial, in his closing argument, the previous defense attorney said something along the line of, "Ladies and gentlemen, I don't know why these girls are making up these stories, but we know they are." Now, if the defense cannot come up with the reason for the charges, then how can the jury be expected to do so to create reasonable doubt? As I cross-examined the previous lawyer about his statement, the judge interrupted me and said, "Mr. Zaner, if I had criminal charges filed against me, I would hire Mr. Smith to represent me. He's one of the top criminal defense lawyers in this area." My response was, "Well, your honor, if it was a charge of some type of sexual molestation then you would be going to prison because the lawyer didn't understand what had to be done."

131

EXPERTS

In these types of cases, expert witnesses can be very important. As a defense attorney, my job is to find an expert who is familiar with the subject, who has testified and who is going to be straight forward, understandable and honest. The last thing I want to do is hire someone who is strictly there to make a buck and he will say whatever I want him to say. That is the worst kind of expert you can have for your case. You need an expert who is going to be honest as to whether and how he is going to help you. In addition to providing direct testimony, the expert should assist the attorney in preparing the cross-examination of the state's expert witness.

I had a situation in a PCR hearing where I took a video deposition of a state expert who testified around the country on behalf of prosecutors. With the assistance of my expert, I understood the science so well that by the time I was done with my examination of this particular expert, he was not only agreeing with what I was asking him, he was also asking for our research. Ideally, you and your expert become a team. You need to work with your expert and he needs to work with you. You should meet with your expert so that both of you are on the same page in regard to direct questioning and cross-examination.

Sometimes you have a case where things are far from ordinary even though it might initially appear to be a clear-cut case. As a defense attorney, you must be willing to look outside the box and not simply handle it as a run-of-the-mill case. You never know what is there. A few years ago, I had a situation where a woman was accused of putting her child in scalding water because the child had what looked like an immersion burn. During our investigation, we discovered that the child had eaten some Ex-Lax when the child was with the babysitter.

We performed research and found a doctor who had written an article about people being falsely accused of immersion burn and child-endangerment in this very situation. There is a chemical component in Ex-Lax that, when the child passes bodily waste, will burn the child's skin and leave marks that appear as if the child had been put in scalding water. I presented all the documentation and pictures to the expert. He reviewed it, and based on his report, the charges were dismissed and the mother was reunited with her child. This is a classic example of the lawyer and the expert working as a successful team.

Your lawyer needs to look outside the box, and the client can help the lawyer do this. The lawyer needs to be willing to work with his client. No one knows everything and lawyers who believe they know everything are probably not willing to listen. If they are not willing to change or not willing to look at everything that is or could be behind the charges, then you should run away because I certainly would if it were me. Just because a lawyer has a good reputation does not mean that he knows how to handle these types of cases.

When it comes to the other half of the defense team, the expert, it is important to look for any little thing in the expert's background: anything in his history that the prosecutor can use to discredit him and affect his credibility during cross-examination. I have only had this situation happen one time during all my years of practice. An expert did not tell me about something that happened 20 years before that affected his entire background. The prosecutor was able to use that information to attack his credibility and to destroy our case. I asked what I thought were the necessary questions and we did the research, but this was something I could not have found no matter how much I researched. The prosecutor, who has access to more resources and more information, was able to find the damaging information. Therefore, you must be very careful.

There is no substitute for spending the time to be thoroughly prepared and to prepare the expert. The reason these cases are so costly is that experts charge a significant amount of money for their time and for their expertise. Normally, it is difficult, if not impossible, to obtain a local expert. You typically must go out of town, and oftentimes out of state, to find your expert. You then must pay travel expenses and other costs in addition to the expert's hourly fee. It may be costly but if your client is exonerated, it is worth it.

SHAKEN BABY SYNDROME

I have defended several shaken baby cases. I was even asked to appear on "The Montel Williams Show" because a client was found not guilty of murdering her child. These cases are incredibly medically-driven. If you are going to handle one of these cases, you need to be willing to spend an enormous amount of time to learn about the science. The first case I had, I watched more than 70 hours of video tapes of direct and cross-examination testimony of experts in the *au pair* case that Barry Scheck handled a number of years ago. I had experts from around the country provide documentation and information to me. By the time we went to trial and I had to cross-examine the state forensic pathologist, she interrupted me at one point and said, "Mr. Zaner, you sound like a forensic pathologist." I said, "Well, thank you. Would you please answer the question?"

You must be willing to spend the time and your client needs the resources to hire experts that you need. There are some national organizations and trial consultants with whom I work frequently.

The National Child Abuse and Defense Resource Center who has access to numerous experts and are great people to work with. They can help with shaken baby cases but also false allegations in abuse cases. You need to go after every bit of evidence you can. Normally, shaken baby allegations occur when children are very young. You need to get pre-natal records, the mother's medical records and the birthing records.

One of the problems with these cases is that, even today, doctors are taught that if there is evidence of subdural hematomas and/or retinal hemorrhages, then it is automatically shaken baby syndrome. Unfortunately, that is just wrong. The science does not support those conclusions, but that is what they are still taught in medical school today. After one shaken baby trial, my client was found not guilty and the prosecutor's office organized a seminar with numerous experts discussing shaken baby syndrome. Every expert talked about subdural and retinal subdural hemorrhages as being evidence of shaken baby syndrome. I approached a neurosurgeon after he spoke. I said, "Doctor, do me a favor: read this article." He approached me later and said, "You know, that's really interesting. I'm going to have to look into that." How outrageous is it that a lawyer has to tell a neurosurgeon what the science is because the doctor failed to keep up on it.

If you, as a defense attorney, are going to handle a shaken baby case, you need to look at the research and familiarize yourself with all of the other conditions and causes that produce these types of injuries in an infant. I recently had a case in which the prosecutor was claiming my client shook the child. The day of the trial, the prosecution ended up dismissing the case because I had science and experts that proved them wrong. I was prepared to make their expert appear pretty foolish during my cross-examination.

As a layperson, if you find yourself in a situation where you are being accused of shaking your child, *do not talk to the police and do not talk to Protective Services*. If you are at the hospital because your child is in critical care, you cannot talk to them about specifics without your lawyer because they will do everything they can to try to convict you. They believe that you are guilty, especially if retinal hemorrhages and subdural hematomas are present. You must have a lawyer as soon as possible to give you proper advice. However, be very careful. If you go to a lawyer and the lawyer tells you it will cost a few thousand dollars, I can almost guarantee you the lawyer is looking to make a plea bargain and will essentially get some money then sell you out.

Once again, the problem is these cases cost substantial sums of money to defend. For one of the shaken baby cases I handled, I made no money whatsoever. To top that off, I spent $35,000 out of my own pocket for experts because I was not going to let my client be found guilty. Fortunately, she was found not guilty. If you are hiring a lawyer in this area of law, once again, you need to find out what kind of cases he has tried. Learn about his experience and find out if he is a good trial lawyer. Above all else, be sure he really understands the science in this area.

ON THE SUBJECT OF PLEA BARGAINS

These agreements need to be approached with caution. It depends upon what the plea bargain is and how well prepared you are to go to trial. Let's say you do not have the resources for experts, you do not have resources for the other things that you need for a thorough preparation with investigators, and you do not have the ammunition you need. You might say to yourself, "I will go to trial anyway." If so, you will be in a lot of trouble. Of course, you can get on the witness stand and say, "I didn't do it. This is false," but you must understand that these cases are different from other cases. Here, no matter what the law promises, you are clearly presumed guilty the minute the charges are brought against you and you are forced to prove your innocence.

If you do not have the resources and ammunition needed, especially in a shaken baby case—if you cannot afford the experts you need—you are put in a position where you will have no choice but to take a plea bargain. Therefore, it is important that you understand the plea bargain and its ramifications. What does it mean? Do you have to register as a sex offender? How long do you have to register? What does it mean as far as where you can live? How does your plea affect these things?

There are all kinds of collateral consequences in these matters. In fact, some states now are doing something that the courts have upheld as being constitutional. If you enter a plea or go to trial and you are found guilty of a sexual offense, you are labeled a Tier One, Tier Two, or Tier Three sexual offender. You must register as a sex offender for a period of years and, in some states, additional civil commitment proceedings will be filed against you *after* you have completed your prison term. These are civil charges from which the court can determine you have a mental defect and you are a danger to society. As a result, the court has the right to lock you up in a mental institution until such time that you are deemed no longer a danger to society. That could mean the rest of your life.

You might ask, "How can they do that? That's double jeopardy where you can't be tried and punished for the same crime." Well, they can do it because they claim the civil commitment is not criminal and the courts have upheld the ruling. Today, in this country, people who have served 10, 20, or 25 years in prison can then be locked up for the rest of their lives after being released from prison. Plea bargains can carry many hidden consequences. You must consider what the overall effect is going to be on your entire life.

GOING TO TRIAL

Jury Trial Or Bench Trial?

If you cannot come up with an agreement with the prosecution or you have concluded that you want to go to trial, you may have a choice of whether to have a bench trial or jury trial. I practice in Ohio and Michigan and these two states are different. In Ohio, it is the defendant's decision whether he wants a jury trial or a bench trial. On the other hand, in Michigan, both the prosecutor and the defendant must agree if it is to be a bench trial or a jury trial. I do not know about other states so you would need to look at your state's rules and regulations as to how that is determined. It is very rare that I try a case just to the judge when I have the option to try it before a jury because I would rather have one out of twelve or one out of eight be on my side as opposed to only having one person, the judge, decide the guilt or innocence of my client.

Most judges are elected, so they are looking at the publicity factor. There have been occasions when I have tried cases as bench trials for various reasons. The first shaken baby trial I tried was before a judge that I knew from high school. I knew he was intellectually honest and he was a brand-new judge. I agreed to waive the jury and I tried it to the bench. Fortunately, we received a not guilty verdict. I recently had a drug case with a new judge who used to be a prosecutor. We had some negative history. He and I had numerous bouts and did not get along very well but the case involved a legal issue. I tried an aggravated vehicular homicide case, a felony, before him and waived the jury because

138

I thought the case should have been a misdemeanor. That was precisely what the judge did. Both of those situations happen to have panned out, but I know situations where lawyers have waived juries and tried the case before a judge and almost every one of those clients was found guilty.

Jury Selection

Jury selection is another one of the factors that an attorney can develop only through hands-on experience. When I am choosing a jury, as much as the judge will let me, I try to help the jury understand what the defense is trying to argue. Even if it is a false report, these kinds of things become real memories to little children. It is important to try to help the jury understand some of the concepts that you are trying to present. It is important to have the jurors talking to each other. During jury selection, you should not be lecturing. You want to hear what the jurors have to say, because that is how you find out the information you need about them. One of the best things that can happen is that a juror says something absolutely off-the-wall with which you do not necessarily agree. You cannot chastise the juror. That is a mistake, but these are the kinds of things you need to know *before* this juror becomes a part of your jury. You want to encourage all the jurors to be honest and you do that by appreciating the comments that each juror makes so you can obtain information. Jury selection is challenging.

I have used jury consultants before and it is still a matter of feel. You just never know what you are going to get, no matter what questions you ask, because jurors are not necessarily 100% honest with you. I had a jury trial where the jury was hung, 11 to 1, for not guilty. After the trial ended, six or seven of the jurors came up to me stating they were very angry with the one juror who held out because she had been molested when she was a youth and she had denied that when we asked her questions about it during jury selection. The juror froze up when the child testified and she would not listen to anything else that was presented during the trial.

No matter how much you do or how much you try, you may get that kind of juror. All you can do is your best. Many times, you run across what we call "stealth jurors." During selection, these folks are going to say whatever you want to hear because they have an agenda and they want very badly to be on that jury. You just do the best you can to try to figure that out and try not to allow them to sit on your jury.

Cross Examination

During cross-examination, I normally do all the testifying. What I mean by that is that I will ask questions which have yes or no responses because I know what I want from the witness. I want to keep the witness on a short leash. I do not want to give the witness an opportunity to expand on questions or to throw things in that are not responsive to questions. Cross-examination is an art. You need to know what you are doing and where you are going with each question. I have seen lawyers write out all their questions. In my opinion, that is a mistake because if you are writing out questions, all you are doing is waiting for them to finish so that you can get into your next question. A good defense attorney will listen to what the witness says because there may be an entirely different area of questions you want to ask based on the answers to your previous questions. Perhaps you get new information or the witness gives you the opportunity to ask a question you were waiting to ask. Writing out questions and following a script is a big mistake. Outlines of areas for cross examination is better.

The same thing is true with opening and closing statements. You can certainly have notes and an outline, but to write your opening or closing statement means you are going to read it to the jury. That is not effective and is certainly neither impressive nor persuasive. It is vital that you engage and persuade the jury. You need to get up before the jury and talk to the jury. You need to make eye contact with them. You want them listening and following what you are saying.

Sometimes, there is more than one defense attorney present at the defense table—remember OJ's legal team? I believe it is a mistake for the attorneys to split up *voir dire*, opening statement, and closing statement. *Voir dire* is the opportunity that you have to connect with the jury. You want them to like you, believe you, and trust you. Why would you want someone else to take the opening or closing statement? To my way of thinking, the person who does the *voir dire* and chooses the jury has to give the opening and closing statements. You can certainly split up who questions the witnesses but, in my opinion, there should be one lawyer who handles the *voir dire*, opening statement, and closing statement.

THE FINAL WORD

I often receive calls from lawyers who ask me to assist them, talk to them, and give them suggestions. I have lectured on the subject of bad interviewing techniques and false allegations around the country. I have done so a number of times, so lawyers from around the country know me and contact me. I am more than happy to give advice as to how I think they ought to handle their cases. There are people that I can call to do the same thing. It has been good being on the national level to have these contacts. I know many of the top experts in the country and that gives me extended resources.

I recently spoke at a conference in Las Vegas. If you are a young lawyer and just getting started, you need to talk to somebody. Do not think you know everything. You need to sit down and go through all the issues including not talking to the police, publicity, how to handle the case, how to organize your case, and your theories of your case. As I said, these cases are a different breed, and to be successful, you must know the differences and how to address them. In my career, I learned things from major multi-million dollar divorce cases and malpractice cases to personal injury cases and major civil litigation. I defended a $30 million civil case and have handled major high-profile criminal cases. I have had many types of cases during my career and each case teaches me something different.

My background is in chemical engineering, so science does not scare me. I relish delving into the science and talking with experts in order to develop the things that we need to do in order to defend the case to try to get the best possible result for our client. Recently, I was in a conference call with two experts talking about a case. It was fascinating listening to the doctors and throwing in my two cents' worth. The experts are actually learning things from each other, which is also a fascinating process to be a part of. The bottom line is, if you want to be a good defense lawyer, you always have to be willing to spend the time and be willing to do whatever is necessary to get a just result. A just result is the best result you can ever get for your client.

(This content should be used for informational purposes only. It does not create an attorney-client relationship with any reader and should not be construed as legal advice. If you need legal advice, please contact an attorney in your community who can assess the specifics of your situation.)

7

WHY I DO WHAT I DO

by William DeNardo, Esq.

William DeNardo, Esq.
Law Office of William DeNardo
Plymouth Meeting, Pennsylvania
www.williamdenardolaw.com

As a criminal defense attorney practicing across several counties in the Southern Pennsylvania area, William DeNardo is known as a top-notch legal mind. After graduating from Widener School of Law in 1997, he began his career as an Assistant District Attorney in Pennsylvania's Montgomery County. William entered private practice in 2001 and has been successfully defending his clients ever since.

William is an experienced litigator who is passionate about his craft. He is respected by local police, the bench and bar. He has been recognized both locally and nationally for excellence in his field of criminal defense. He enjoys the challenge of the job, the adversarial nature of the work and the opportunity to advise and counsel his clients.

WHY I DO WHAT I DO

"So, what's it like defending the bad guys?" "Why did you leave the prosecutor's office to join the 'Dark Side'?" I get asked these questions from time to time, usually from well meaning, genuinely curious folks. When asked, I have to remind myself to take a breath and recognize they are not trying to be offensive. People sometimes forget that we, thankfully, live in a society where the accused is presumed to be innocent and is entitled to a defense. I recognize that not everyone understands the role of the criminal defense attorney and why I do what I do. Candidly, this is not something I envisioned doing growing up. I am glad, however, that it has I found my way into, what I believe to be, the most challenging and rewarding field of practice.

When I was a kid, my grandfather told me that the key to happiness and success was figuring out what you were good at and then making a living doing it. Simple enough advice, right?

In my formative years, I learned that I like thinking on my feet. I liked watching trial attorneys work at their craft on television shows; some great movies encapsulated the appeal of being a trial attorney. The idea of waking up every morning and not knowing how the day's events would unfold or what kind of adventures you'd get into appealed to me.

I went to college in the Midwest. I came back to Philadelphia during my junior year at college for a program that allowed me to intern at the Philadelphia district attorney's office for a semester. While there, I was fortunate to work and observe some extremely talented trial attorneys working in very difficult circumstances as prosecutors. I was immediately bitten by the bug.

I set a goal to become a trial lawyer. Public speaking and confrontation did not scare me. I knew it was a tough job and required a lot of commitment. Years of playing competitive sports trained me to know how to put your head down and persevere. I went to on to law school. I interned every summer at the district attorney's office in Philadelphia. After graduation, I became a prosecutor in suburban Philadelphia, and had my first jury trial within eight months of becoming a licensed attorney. During the three and a half years that I served as a county prosecutor, I handled a variety of cases, from driving under the influence to homicide, and everything in between.

As an assistant district attorney, I was responsible for making sure that justice was done. I realized that the role of the defense attorney was an integral component in the administration of justice. The defense attorneys I dealt with fought hard for their clients. They held my feet to the proverbial fire as a prosecutor. They made sure that I did my job as a prosecutor and made me strive to do the right thing every time. I left the prosecutor's office with a tremendous respect for my adversaries.

My experiences with the defense bar influenced me to become a defense attorney immediately after leaving the prosecutor's office. For me, becoming a defense attorney was a natural progression from the role of a prosecutor. A defense attorney starts with the same subject matter, but progresses differently. It was a different side of the table—a different argument, and a completely different perspective.

It's the adversarial nature of being a defense attorney that I like best. I like thinking on my feet and preparing a defense for a client. I like the investigative aspect of this type of work. Being a defense attorney gives me the ability to have a one-on-one relationship with the client, somebody who is accused of doing something serious, who has trepidation about their future. That person turns to you, their defense attorney, to be their advocate, ally, and advisor. That's not something you get as a prosecutor.

That can be an empowering thing. Obviously, it can be stressful, and it's a staggering responsibility — somebody's wellbeing is in your hands — but it brings out the best in me. It brings out the best in any good defense attorney.

I've described my job to people in this way: think of me as a "paratrooper" lawyer. I fly around the stratosphere until a call comes from a client who needs me. I parachute into the middle of the mess, which is really the beginning of the process of any kind of criminal representation. My job is to find out where the battle lines are and to get the situation on an even keel so we can start working our way forward. Not everybody gets that kind of drama in their everyday work. It's exciting and I like that.

TYPES OF CLIENTS

As American citizens, we have rights. We are innocent until proven guilty. We generally have the right to be tried by a jury.

The burden is either on the Commonwealth, the state, or the federal government (depending on the jurisdiction of the prosecutor) to prove your guilt in a criminal case "beyond a reasonable doubt." The burden is not there by accident; it's there by design. If your liberty is at stake, then the case against you must be incredibly strong and proven by capable hands.

Generally speaking, two types of people come to see me. Some clients come in and say, "I did it—I'm nervous about what's in store for me, and I'm concerned about going to jail for a long time. I'm concerned about losing my job, family, income, and pension, etc." I consider these people to be 'damage-control' clients. My representation would be focused on controlling the damage in their case. This requires me to work with the prosecutor in an effort to try and negotiate a fair disposition of their case. That usually translates into trying to get my client less jail time, less probation, lower fines, etc.

The other type of client comes in and says, "I didn't do any of this. I am being railroaded. They got the wrong person. This is motivated by some other reason. I have to be free of this offense." With these types of clients, I take the case to the mat and try to get an acquittal.

Over the years, I've observed some of the most vocal critics of criminal defense ("How could you do what you do?") when their family member gets arrested or charged with a crime—they cannot get ahold of me fast enough. "Bill, you're not going to believe this. My nephew got arrested. I need your help right away." Of course I'll help them, but in my mind, I laugh and think, "Wait a second. You're the person who always says, 'How can you represent the bad guys?'"

WHY HIRE AN ATTORNEY?

In Pennsylvania, an individual has the right to defend himself. There is no mandatory requirement for them to be represented by counsel; I've seen individuals represent themselves. I generally do not think that is a good idea. One Judge I know likes to tell non-represented defendants: "Look. When I get a cavity, I don't try to fill my own cavity. When I need a root canal, I don't try to do my own root canal. This is a serious thing you are about to undertake. You don't have the training, expertise, or the experience to deal with it. It is in your best interest to have a defense attorney represent you." That's a pretty good analogy.

Certainly, there are aspects of this work that don't require heavy-duty intellectual capabilities, while other aspects require the help of a seasoned defense attorney. Good defense attorneys are skilled questioners and cross-examiners; we are able to synthesize information and organize it in a law-friendly fashion that can be presented to a jury in fairly short order. We have the confidence and the ability to speak on our feet. We don't shy away from the stage that is the courtroom, if you will; we embrace the limelight. We work at the skill of persuasion constantly. At the end of the day in this business, in a trial setting, the results rest on the person who the jury trusts and believes. Do they believe you as the accused, or do they believe the Commonwealth or the State in the form of the prosecutor?

You want your advocate to know and understand the law and also be familiar with the rules of governance surrounding court procedures.. It's also essential that your advocate has the ability and the charisma to communicate well — one who is not only personable, but who can also gain the respect of the fact-finders (the judge and the jury). That is something that a good defense attorney can provide.

If a defendant represents himself and that doesn't work out well, it can bring financial and social ruin down upon him. The accused can lose his job, his liberty, and his ability to generate future income because of the conviction on his record. He may be able to mitigate or completely avoid all of those things by the representation of a trained, experienced defense attorney.

CHOOSING AN ATTORNEY

There are many desirable qualities to look for in a defense attorney. One of the most important requirements is to have an attorney who is accessible. I give my clients my email address and my cell phone number; I return my clients' emails, phone calls, and texts. I'm accessible 24/7. If a client is reaching out to me on a Sunday night it usually because he is in major trouble, not because he wants to chat. If I had a problem taking those calls I would stop being a criminal defense attorney and become a banker. If your defense attorney is tied up in court or otherwise occupied when you call, it's not an unreasonable expectation to hear back from him within a 24-hour period. If a professional won't return your call, that's a problem. You may have the wrong person representing you.

As far as time and fee scheduling, my practice is generally flat-fee based, so the client doesn't have to worry about the clock or phone calls costing money. That serves the client, and it's good for the lawyer as well. To me, your problem is like a project. In the beginning, I tell you what the project costs. If it takes 100 hours to get it done, you don't have to worry about your bill. That's already included in what you're paying me.

As far as payment structures and ease of making payments, I give my clients the option of paying me with credit cards. Not many defense attorneys accept that method of payment, and I frankly don't understand why not. I also try to make it easier on clients by offering payment plans. This typically translates to a portion of the total retainer fee upfront followed by the balance at a later, agreed upon, date. I understand cash flow. Understandably, sometimes people need time to get their money together, but they'll start with a deposit. That's another thing to consider. Is your attorney willing to work with you on a payment structure?

I give a free consultation, which should be expected by any defense client. In my business, it's a pleasure to sit down with people and talk about the case in a free consultation. By the end of the consult, I like to tell people, "I want to be able to give you a best case scenario, the worst case scenario, and what's in between. I'll tell you what I can do for you and what it's going to cost." If we come to a meeting of minds, and they want to retain me, we get that done. If not, we shake hands and wish each other luck.

From a big-picture perspective, it's important to have a criminal defense attorney who is not afraid to do his job: be your advocate, cross-examine police officers, make uncomfortable arguments against the DA, and be the wheel that squeaks. It's also important to find an attorney who isn't a one-trick pony. In other words, he isn't just the squeaky wheel. A good attorney should have the ability to negotiate and a sense about when to pull back and let the hand play itself—to know when to ease off the pressure.

When I was a DA, it was much harder to say no to defense attorneys who were respected. It was obvious that they did their job exceedingly well and fought for the client without being jerks all the time. That was an important lesson to learn—you do get more bees with honey than vinegar. It's important if you can sense the kind of person that you're dealing with when hiring an attorney. Is this the type of person who has the backbone to stand up and fight the fight, along with the finesse and charisma to get people to listen to him on your behalf?

If you're too nice or too soft in this business, you'll get rolled over. The DA probably won't respect you. If you do not try cases, if you don't litigate things, if you don't keep your edges sharp, a DA won't take you seriously when you start to threaten a trial. As a potential client, those are the things you need to look at. Read the review websites; word-of-mouth is obviously a great barometer of an attorney's reputation. I have told potential clients, "If you need to know more about me, call the district attorney's office, call the local police, and mention my name. See if they have any thoughts about me: good, better, or indifferent. I stand by my reputation."

As a potential client, these are some fair questions to ask: "What kind of experience do you have? Tell me about your background. Have you ever handled cases like mine? If so, how many times? Have you dealt with this police department before? Have you dealt with this judge? Have you dealt with this DA's office before? How do you get paid?" Clients should know these things about their attorney.

Speaking for myself, I will not handle a case that is outside of my geographical comfort zone, far away from my office. Not only does it burn a great deal of travel time, it is also important for a defense attorney to establish a relationship within the local justice system. I don't think it is practical advocacy for an attorney to go too far afield; it is better for a criminal defense attorney to know the area that concerns their clients' interests. In that case, I'm much happier referring a potential client to a local counselor, although not every attorney does that.

When you're trying to get a feeling about an attorney, there are more delicate questions to ask: "Are they capable of trying the case? Are they capable of negotiating?" As a client, you also should be able to get a sense that the person you're talking to has passion about what he or she is doing. Passion is important. I'm blessed to be able to make a living doing something I really enjoy doing; I think that permeates my practice. If their passion about what they do is clear and obvious, that's a good sign for a potential client.

PREPARING FOR TRIAL

Part of my job is understanding how juries work. In my opinion, juries want to believe the Commonwealth or the State. A jury sees the prosecutor as the good guy or girl, the one wearing the "white hat," because they are wearing the proverbial white hats. As protectors of the public, they should be meting out justice. Since juries don't expect their employees—the police and prosecutors— to not do a good job, it's human nature for them to believe that the accused did something very wrong. They will look at the accused and wonder, "What did that person do to warrant this trial where we sit as jury?" You have to know that up front.

A defense attorney must persuade people to open up their minds beyond that initial mistrust of their client. Obviously, it's important for the jury to like the defense attorney, which is just old-fashioned charisma: some have it, some don't. At a minimum, they need to respect the attorney and his abilities, listen carefully to the statements he's making, and listen to the questions he's asking. A good defense attorney will always remind the jury that an accusation is just an accusation and that his or her client sits before them an innocent person, as innocent as the jury members themselves.

Speaking as an attorney, the way to achieve a lot of that is to be good at what you do—by "good," I mean "thoroughly prepared." When an attorney enters the courtroom, he is being measured. He has to be polished and he must exude confidence. These qualities give the impression of a person who is obviously in control. Human beings like to know that somebody's got a handle on the crisis at hand. I write out a script for most of my trials. As in professional sports, practice is the hardest part, so I will sit down and prepare before making the presentation at court. The preparation and the practice should be grueling so that the trial will flow smoothly.

It's also very much like putting on a stage production. For an attorney, there's a lot of time spent in planning if you want the end result to be powerful. You spend time thinking about your case. You write out questions and outline potential arguments based on how you believe the evidence will flow. You line up your evidence ducks in a row. You memorize your opening statement, you don't stand in front of the jury and read to them from a legal pad. You think about the spot in the courtroom where you're going to ask questions, and how you're going to direct the jury's attention. All of these things are important because you want that jury to believe that "this guy has his stuff together." That can add to your credibility; ultimately, it trickles down to your client's advantage.

The final closing argument is your chance as the defense attorney to let it all hang out and to really shine. At a minimum, you hope that the jury will see and feel your passion and realize that you deserve their attention and your client deserves their best. Ideally you want to use the closing argument as the final act of the "performance" they just sat through. You want it to resonate and start their deliberations with what you just laid out for them in your closing.

JURY SELECTION

First of all, the ability to have a jury is probably the most important aspect of the criminal justice system in the United States. We have the amazing ability to have twelve citizens weigh the evidence; these are people who don't know you, who don't know the DA, and who are not necessarily lawyers or judges. They just listen to the testimony and make a determination. It's a very powerful thing. It's especially remarkable when you compare it to some of the other systems in the world.

There's even a screening process to ensure everyone's ability. Screening ensures that the members of the jury are fair and unbiased, will follow the judge's instruction on the law, and will keep an open mind. That process is called *voir dire*, which means a series of questions and answers that are asked of jurors. Defense and Commonwealth attorneys use the answers to those questions to determine whether the potential juror could be fair and impartial. Will he or she be a good person to sit in judgment on the case?

People who have physical problems and handicaps, or those whose major life events would make it impossible for them to sit as jurors are often struck from the jury panel. Other issues might include the potential juror's way of answering questions that would indicate a personal issue with sitting as a juror, or the fact that they can't follow the judge's instruction, or a hint that they don't believe the defendant simply because he or she is the defendant. Sometimes people don't believe police officers just because they're police officers. Those individuals are typically questioned for further details. The attorneys have the ability to question them and determine where their biases and prejudices lie, and whether or not they could be very fair and impartial.

Once that process is over, the Defense and the Commonwealth go through a series of strikes. They are given the ability to strike a potential jury member from that jury panel for any reason other than race. As a defense attorney, your client is part of the process. You are taking calculated risks and/or educated guesses and much of that depends on your gut feeling as to whom you absolutely do not want on a jury of your clients' peers. It is obviously an inexact science, to put it mildly.

In Pennsylvania, this happens relatively quickly. In a more serious case, such as a capital murder case, finding a qualified jury is a much longer process. One of the misnomers about the jury selection process is that you pick who you want on the jury. The truth is both sides get rid of jurors they don't want on their jury. The final twelve become the jury. It's the process of elimination.

The jury represents the law. The judge is the referee. The judge decides what evidence can come in and what evidence stays out. At the end of the day, that jury is the body that decides whether or not the prosecution has proven the case. They listen to the facts during the trial and are instructed on the law by the judge at the conclusion of closing arguments. The jury is then dismissed to begin their deliberations. Ultimately, they are tasked to determine whether or not the prosecutor met that legal obligation and proved their case beyond a reasonable doubt. An attorney's defense will pivot upon that. He should be mindful of the jury, what they're thinking, and where they're looking. He should cater to them to the best of his abilities.

THE OPENING STATEMENT

In Pennsylvania, the opening statement of the Defense always comes after the Commonwealth's opening statement. The trial starts after the jury has been selected, with the prosecutor standing in front of the twelve jurors, telling those twelve jurors that the presented case will prove that the defendant did something illegal. They will prove it beyond a reasonable doubt. In an opening statement, it is impermissible to argue; in other words, you can't make argumentative statements at that time. Sometimes the prosecutor will go out there, usually unintentionally, and begin to argue; this is something that a defense attorney should listen for because it should be met with an objection.

A good defense attorney and a good prosecutor will both structure their opening statement and use language within it in such a way that is argumentative without technically being an argument. At the end of a prosecutor's opening statement, a prosecutor wants that jury to be unanimously ready to convict. A prosecutor hopes that the jurors don't want to hear anything else from the defense attorney or anything else from witnesses because they just heard the prosecutor. They believe the prosecutor and they simply want to convict right this minute. That's how persuasive an opening statement ought to be.

As a defense attorney, my job is to take those bullets that the prosecutor fires and get the jury to think about each one of them. "Listen to ME now." In my opening statement, I try to cast some doubt over the prosecutor's theory of the case. In my opening, I want the jury to begin to question what the prosecution just told them. "Wait a second. There's more to the story that the DA didn't cover in his opening statement. I don't like that. I don't like that the DA is now trying to be sneaky about this."

I like to try to anticipate an opening statement from the DA. That's not difficult since the evidence will speak for itself. The opening statement for the prosecution is usually an overview of what the evidence will show.

I try to make an educated guess about how the prosecution will show their hand, like in a poker game: which part of the case will the DA highlight, and which part will they either downplay or not mention, as they try to steer the attention of the jury? By way of example, in a typical opening, I like to say, "You just heard the prosecutor say X and Y and Z. What you didn't hear the prosecutor mention was this:

1. There's not a single fingerprint left at the scene that comes from my client's hand,

2. There's not a single piece of scientific evidence, DNA, or blood results. I ran through every single scientific test that I can think of, linking my client to the scene, and

3. There's not a single eyewitness to put my client at that place.

Yet despite all that, they want you to believe that my client did it.

Why?"

If I can highlight the areas that the prosecutor doesn't want to touch, that is a powerful thing in an opening statement. It gets the fact finder (the jury) to learn something new about the case, and makes them wonder why the DA didn't tell them. The response that an attorney hopes for is "the prosecutor thinks we're dumb, and that offends us." Now you've got their attention.

CROSS-EXAMINATION

Cross-examination is a skill and an art. It's important for a skilled, experienced defense attorney to know that cross-examination is one of the best tools in the defense arsenal. However, it's like old dynamite. Be careful how you use it, or it could blow up in your face.

When a witness testifies, the party who calls the witness in a criminal case must ask direct questions. They have to ask open-ended questions that invite the witness to answer however they want to answer. They are not allowed to lead the witness to a certain answer with their question.

Cross-examination of that same witness by the other side is exactly the opposite scenario. Most all of the questions should be leading questions. Cross-examination is the covert opportunity for the questioner to testify without actually testifying. During cross-examination, the questioner is subtly telling the jury what he believes this case is about, how he believes this witness should be testifying, or what really happened. He's not really giving the witness the opportunity to explain his answers—to explain anything—beyond the questions that are specifically asked. It's a defense attorney's method to take control of a witness who is testifying in a way that the DA wants to use against the defendant.

Cross-examination is a very powerful tool for the defense attorney. By its very nature, it can be uncomfortable for the witness. As a result, an attorney must be able to anticipate that the witnesses won't like answering only "yes" or "no" to the questions. They frequently feel threatened by the questions and especially the way in which you are asking those questions.

In movies and TV shows, you see grisly cross-examinations. I find that tactic to often times be ineffective. "Badgering" cross-examinations can blow up in your face as a defense attorney. If you do take on a witness during cross-examination and they don't like how you're "coming at them," they will shut down. They will force out answers that are not really answers to the questions. Their response will make you look like, at best, a jerk. Perhaps worse, you may look like an ineffective, pathetic loser of an attorney who has to beg the judge to order the witness to answer your questions in front of a jury. Neither of those scenarios are what you want in front of a jury. They undermine your efforts. You strive to be the person in control.

That said, there are times when it's necessary to go after a witness on cross examination.. However, I'd much rather have a witness, even in cross-examination, feel comfortable in giving you unbiased, honest, or unfiltered answers. You can ask a very difficult question in a way that doesn't sound threatening. Not everybody can do that, but it is one of the marks of a good defense attorney. The witness should be able to open up to you and ultimately give you what is hopefully the truth. Then, in closing arguments, you synthesize that with other information. If you really want to take apart a witness in front of the jury, do it during the closing. The witness can's take you on in your closing argument. Let the jury know that the witness in question is no good and they should not believe a word they say.

CLOSING ARGUMENT

The closing argument is the grand finale of your production. In Pennsylvania, the defense attorney goes first. It's your opportunity to argue on behalf of your client, to take the gloves off and tell the jury what the case shows, within the boundaries.

You can make arguments, poke holes in the prosecution's case, attack witnesses, and praise other witnesses. You want to get the jury to think about the evidence in a new way that they haven't thought about until that point. The jury should be thinking and talking about what you said as they go back to deliberate. "The defense counsel said that witness might be testifying this way because she is best friends with the victim. Do you think that's possible?" You want them to be able to walk away saying, "Hmm. I'm going to have to think about that a little bit." It's especially important to make an impact, because the prosecution gets to go last; they get the last word.

Again, I like to script as much as possible in a trial. Closing arguments however are un-scriptable. The closing argument is an organic thing. Your ability to passionately argue in the closing is the ribbon on the gift box that neatly ties up the case. If you have a theory in your case, that's when it all comes together and sets, like concrete. Sometimes, the jury sits through the case without being exactly sure where it's all going, though they're following the law. In the closing argument, you try to connect the dots and demonstrate that the Commonwealth and the prosecutor did not prove the case beyond a reasonable doubt.

THE VERDICT OR NOT

In order to be convicted in Pennsylvania, all twelve jury members must unanimously agree that the Commonwealth (represented by the prosecutor) has proven their case against the accused beyond a reasonable doubt. Conversely, in order for the defendant to be acquitted or found not guilty, all twelve members of that jury must unanimously agree that the prosecutor did not prove their case against the defendant beyond a reasonable doubt. If there's a split, if even one member of the jury holds a differing opinion from the majority, the court declares a mistrial as a result of the jury being hung.

At some point during the deliberations, the judge asks the jury if they could come to a unanimous conclusion. If the answer is no, the judge then brings out the jury, and instructs them to keep deliberating with an open mind and work towards a resolution. If a period of time goes by after that and the jury still cannot come to a resolution, the judge would find the jury to be a hung jury and would declare a mistrial. This simply means that the jury was unable to come to a conclusion and they're going to start the whole process all over again. A retrial will be scheduled with a new jury and everyone goes through all of the steps a second time.

Generally speaking, I believe that the Defense has the advantage on the second time around, especially because there's no compulsion to present any evidence in favor of the defendant; it's up to the Commonwealth to prove their case. The prosecution typically doesn't change their approach because they are the charging party; the facts and the evidence have not changed. They're playing their best hand from the beginning. The prosecution can't hide evidence. It's fully open to disclosure or discovery. Typically, I know about everything in the Commonwealth's arsenal prior to the trial. In contrast to television shows, in the real world, there are almost never "surprise" witnesses or evidence.

However, sometimes events turn out differently in the second trial in contrast to the first trial. For instance, a witness for the Commonwealth may testify in a certain way at the first trial, but in the second trial, they start to testify differently. That creates a chink in the Commonwealth's armor. When this happens, the defense counsel has the opportunity to impeach that testimony—

to cross-examine those witnesses in a way that points out the inconsistencies in their testimony. You ask them: "You testified this way a month ago. Now you're testifying this way. Why is that? Which story is true? Are you trying to benefit the Commonwealth by changing your story?"

The Commonwealth has many witnesses on record under oath after a trial. In the second trial they have to testify again. The prosecutor worries not so much about the police officer, but the civilian witnesses who can be loose cannons. When they testify differently the second time around, it creates an opening for a skilled defense attorney to paint their testimony as less than credible.

When does the Commonwealth use its resources to take the case to court a second time? If it's a serious case that the government feels strongly about, enough to take the case to trial in the first place, they will take it back to court. If it's a serious charge, especially if people have been hurt, it's more likely than not that the government will take up the case again and restart the whole process. If it is a less serious offense or a case without injured victims, the government tries to look at it objectively. At that point, they may realize that the case is not strong. It is in their best interest, at that point, to approach the defense counsel with an offer to negotiate a plea bargain deal for your client's consideration.

Prosecutors generally don't like to lose—nobody does—so the potentially weak cases will often be dealt away or plea-bargained prior to taking the case to trial. If the case really does go to trial, odds are that the prosecutor feels very strongly about it. It's a non-negotiable case. Eventually, the time may come (after a first or second mistrial) when the Commonwealth realizes that they can't prove the case convincingly or beyond a reasonable doubt. At that point, the case usually gets withdrawn.

Ideally, as a client, you've taken the time to go to court and watch these people in action so that you can see and appreciate some of the qualities that all good defense attorneys have and use. For me, being in court and using my skills as my clients' advocate, to act as their mouthpiece, is a powerful thing. I love what I do. I'm passionate about what I do, and my results speak for themselves. There are a lot of ways to practice law. Most of them don't interest me. This kind of work interests me because it's important to do. Every day, I get to help a lot of people who are in difficult circumstances; in and of itself, that is extremely fulfilling.

8

EVERY CITIZEN DESERVES THE BEST DEFENSE AND IS CONSIDERED INNOCENT UNTIL PROVEN GUILTY

by Jeremiah D. Allen, Esq.

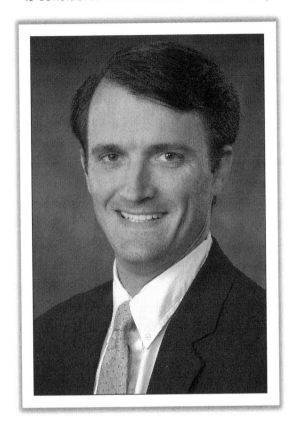

Jeremiah D. Allen, Esq.
Law Office of Jeremiah D. Allen, P.A.
Orlando, Florida
www.jeremiahdallen.com

Jeremiah Allen was born in Orlando, Florida as a fourth generation Floridian. He did his undergraduate work at the University of the South in Sewanee, Tennessee and later earned his law degree at the Appalachian School of Law in Grundy, Virginia.

In the years following law school, attorney Allen served as an Assistant State Attorney in Clearwater, Florida for approximately 6 years. There he prosecuted cases involving such crimes as driving under the influence, drug trafficking, aggravated battery, manslaughter, and murder. This prosecutorial experience gives him the background to defend those who come to him now, in his criminal defense practice, affording his clients the winning edge that only experience can bring.

EVERY CITIZEN DESERVES THE BEST DEFENSE AND IS CONSIDERED INNOCENT UNTIL PROVEN GUILTY

Sometimes criminal defense lawyers get a bad rap. People see them as slippery, oily guys who go around defending the guilty and getting bad guys out jail. The truth is that the job of a criminal defense attorney is absolutely not to determine the guilt or innocence of the client. In the bigger picture, there is a larger concern. Our criminal justice system follows a constitutional mandate that insists everybody needs to be considered innocent until they are proven guilty in a court of law. The other part of that mandate is that each citizen deserves the best defense possible. In that system, some lawyers have to prosecute, and some lawyers have to defend. Really, the job of a criminal defense attorney is twofold—to make sure that the prosecution is doing their job and that the defendant's constitutional rights are thoroughly protected.

The government is represented by the prosecutor. His job is to ensure that they can prove the case beyond a reasonable doubt. When our founding fathers wrote the Constitution, they believed that it was better for the guilty man to go free than for the innocent to be convicted. In the words of John Adams, "We are to look upon it as more beneficial, that many guilty persons should escape unpunished, than one innocent person should suffer."[1] As criminal defense attorneys, we do have a duty to uphold the Constitution. Of course, we want to do that ethically and responsibly and not perpetrate fraud upon the court, but we generally want to make sure that the rights of the accused are protected — that we do not have innocent people locked up with their liberties taken away.

I became a defense attorney because I've always been drawn to the underdogs. Like cheering for a specific team in sports, or having a passion for protecting people who may not have anyone else to turn to, I personally like representing individuals rather than any large government entity or corporation. I was a prosecutor for a number of years, but I much prefer a one-on-one approach. I like working for individuals rather than being part of an entire governmental machine.

I became a lawyer because I wanted to represent people, know them, and know their family. I can say from experience, when you help an individual who stumbles into a difficult legal situation, it can be very gratifying, much more than representing the government as a prosecutor. Part of being a defense attorney includes having an appreciation for our U.S. Constitution, for our constitutional rights; you don't want to see any individual deprived of his rights. You want to be an advocate for those who may have had their constitutional rights violated.

This seems to be an important role in my life. When I was growing up, I had an older brother who was deaf and blind, so I always thought of myself as a defender of the defenseless. Our family always had difficulties finding schools for him or helping him with the hurdles and difficulties of life in general. When my brother was younger, we used to stand behind him as his advocates to make sure that he had the right supervision and the right education. In my world now, a client almost becomes like a family member—I have the mentality of looking out for them and I enjoy being the advocate for that person.

Some lawyers belong to huge law firms and represent large corporations and insurance companies, which is fine; we need those lawyers too. Other attorneys prefer a more personal connection with the clients. It's rewarding when clients come into your office, and they're interacting with you, and you see their legal troubles through to the end. You get a real connection and a reward for the efforts you make on their behalf.

HOW TO FIND A CRIMINAL DEFENSE LAWYER

If you're in a position to need legal help in a criminal matter, you want to know as much about your new criminal defense attorney as possible. Obviously, you will want to check into his background. Look at his work experience. Has he ever been a prosecutor? Was she a public defender, or did she work for a larger firm under the observation of an older attorney? As a former prosecutor, I've spent about six years at the state attorney's office here in Florida. That experience gives you, number one, a lot of trial jury practice as well as investigation experience. It gives you a greater understanding about the amount and the level of investigation that is required in a criminal case. It also gives you a feel for what separates a good case from a bad case. That's obviously very helpful experience as an attorney defending people's rights.

The second thing to look into would be their trial results. How often have they gone to a jury trial and/or bench trial, and what were the results? How many cases have they taken to trial in the past few months or years? Your case won't necessarily be taken to trial. However, you do want to be certain that this criminal defense attorney has the necessary skills for a trial if you can't come to an agreement with the prosecution and it's necessary to go to court. More specifically, it's important to know the amount of experience that this lawyer has had with your type of case. For example, if you have been charged with DUI, you'll want somebody who understands that particular system.

So, it'll probably be necessary to ask some questions. Does this lawyer handle more criminal matters than civil matters? It is important to know if the lawyer has been more focused on violent crimes rather than white-collar crimes, or has more experience in federal court rather than in state court. It is also important to know if this lawyer does 50-50 criminal defense, or 50% criminal defense and 50% family law.

Also, before hiring a qualified criminal defense attorney, ask if he'll be the lawyer handling your case. Will that person be the one actually taking the case to court or will the firm have an associate handle the case? How much access will you have to the lawyer? When questions or concerns come up, it's important to know if you will have a direct line to that criminal defense attorney or if you will have to go through an associate or legal assistant.

THE DIFFERENCE BETWEEN CIVIL AND CRIMINAL LAW

It's important to make sure that the attorney has a background in criminal law rather than civil law, which has a lower standard of the burden of proof. In civil law, the "plaintiff" (person bringing the lawsuit) only has to prove the facts in the case by preponderance of the evidence. In criminal law, the government (generally in state court or the state attorney's office) brings the charges. They will have to prove their case beyond a reasonable doubt, which is a much higher standard than preponderance of the evidence. Defendants also have more constitutional protections in a criminal case; for instance, there's the right to remain silent. The state or the prosecution cannot compel you, as an individual accused of the crime, to take the stand or to give any statement. In a criminal case, you're not required to prove your own innocence; that burden is placed on the government or the state.

Also, in a civil case, an individual (i.e., the victim of a crime or a wrong) who is intent on monetary damages brings the lawsuit through the court system. In a criminal case, it's the government entity, such as the state of Florida, who would be the "person" bringing those charges; even if the victim of the crime does not want to go forward with the prosecution, the state or the government on their own can go forward with the charges without that person's permission.

This issue comes up many times in domestic matters, in which someone's arrested for domestic battery. The prosecution or the state goes forward with the charges but the victim (or the battered person) won't have anything to do with the case; they're not cooperative. This does make it very difficult on the prosecution, but they still have the choice and the ability to go forward and charge someone with that crime. Even though the victim can't be forced to testify, at a minimum, he or she can be required to show up in court after the prosecution has issued a subpoena to that victim. This can be a stressful situation for everyone involved.

THE EXPENSE OF DEFENSE

Of course, the cost of your defense will be important to you. Generally, though there are many factors, the cost for your lawyer will depend upon the number of hours he'll need to devote to your defense. If the crime is a very serious felony, such as a murder or armed robbery, the lawyer and his firm will need to devote numerous hours preparing for a trial, taking depositions, and doing legal research.

If it's a misdemeanor, first offense, your case will generally take less time than a more serious case with potential prison time or possibly a life sentence. Obviously, the potential cost varies quite a bit. Most of my cases are generally done on a flat fee basis rather than an hourly retainer, as would probably happen in a divorce case. That covers the initial hiring of the lawyer. When you hire your attorney, be very clear about whether or not there will be other fees. Ask whether the fee will be separate from the trial fee and/or a motion fee, or if it's just one flat fee that will cover the entire cost of your representation. You may be able to negotiate those fees when you hire the attorney.

PRIVATE ATTORNEY VS. PUBLIC DEFENDER

Many clients ask this question: "Is there really a difference in the quality of defense you will get from a private attorney or a public defender who is appointed by the court?" That's a good question. I think there may be a few distinctions. Obviously, a public defender will have a much larger caseload than a private attorney; a private attorney will be able to give you very individual attention. He will be able to communicate better with you, as well as with your family. There's also the issue of experience. Some public defenders may have been in the service of the state for many years. In other situations, say if you are charged with a misdemeanor court case in Florida, you will probably get a public defender who's just a few years out of law school, so he's not a fully seasoned lawyer. The lawyer's caseload and experience can be a very big deal. It is important to have an attorney who knows the details of your case and can spend the time explaining all the aspects of your case to you and your family.

If you choose a private lawyer, he's apt to spend more time researching your case. He will really get into the details of your life and the details of your case. Your attorney might hire investigators to track down witnesses or negotiate with the state attorney's office in detail. This kind of involvement can pay off in a big way.

Young lawyers often have their first job working for the government. A large majority of attorneys who are interested in criminal law start out on one of two tracks in the beginning of their careers. Some start out as prosecutor: working with law enforcement, building a case, investigating a case, filing formal charges against people who seem to have committed crimes. In that case, the attorney is a government employee. The prosecutor stereotype is of a rather uptight person who comes from a law enforcement background or family structure.

The second career track is to become a public defender, which also means working for the government. However, this attorney's job is to represent people who don't have the financial ability to hire a private lawyer. A public defender is a tough job because many times it means defending people who don't appreciate your services. Many lawyers that I know, including myself, began on one of these two tracks.

If an attorney starts out as either a public defender or as a prosecutor, he or she will likely begin by handling misdemeanor crimes; in Florida, this means any crime that's punishable by maximum penalty of one year.

As a client, hiring a private attorney can save you lots of money in the long run; one of the best examples that comes immediately to mind is a DUI charge. If you're convicted of DUI in Florida, you will have a huge increase to pay in your insurance. You may be required to get additional separate insurance, insurance requirements that will cost you a lot more money every month; you will have to pay that premium for a long time.

Additionally, a conviction of a criminal charge goes and stays on your permanent record. At least in Florida, there's only one exception to that rule: you may be able to get the case sealed, and then after a period of ten years, expunged. If you are convicted of certain crimes, you're able to have those sealed and/or "expunged," which means that the crimes can be removed from your criminal record. Generally, it must be your first offense or arrest to be sealed and then later expunged. In Florida, "sealing" refers to covering up the crime from the view of the public. At a later time, usually ten years, you can have the case totally expunged from public view in public records, and also from the view of the government or any government entity. Even law enforcement officials might only see some very minimal information, such as the fact of an arrest, and later the fact that it was expunged from public record.

However, for the most part, the record of the crime will never go away. That may hurt your job prospects in the future so that it impacts your potential earnings for a very long time. The prospective employer might be looking at two candidates for a job opening and one has a criminal record and one does not. You're going to be at a disadvantage if you didn't hire the right attorney, or if you just represented yourself and ended up with a criminal conviction on your record. It's worth hiring an experienced and competent counselor to give you good advice on how to handle your criminal case.

WHAT TO EXPECT FROM YOUR CRIMINAL DEFENSE ATTORNEY

Generally, your relationship with your attorney begins with a meeting between the two of you. At this first meeting, you will discuss the facts and details of the case: people who were there, the circumstances of the arrest, any witnesses at the scene, and any available defenses. You'll talk about other items: the fee, the scheduling of the case, the times when you (as the accused) need to appear in court, the times when you don't need to appear in court, the length of time until a trial is set, and the potential penalties involved. As the attorney, usually I give clients a best and worst case scenario. I will also lay out some goals of the case, such as what you have to accomplish and what you think is possible or not possible in a case.

After the initial meeting, a lot of the work will be done by the attorney. He will be reviewing and gathering from the prosecutors what we call "discovery": police reports, witness statements, and any case-related videos. If it's a theft or a DUI, there may be either a surveillance video or a DUI video from the police officer that the attorney will obtain and review. During this time, the defense attorney is also reaching out to any witnesses. As long as the counselor identifies himself as the criminal defense attorney, it's possible for him to ask questions of the alleged victim(s) of the crime. It's important to know what they want to see happen in the case or if they are seeking any out-of-pocket expenses from the accused.

Meanwhile, the prosecutor is also at work building his case against you. Prosecutors generally are given wide latitude in determining the charges that you will face. While law enforcement has already decided if there's probable cause for charging a particular crime, the prosecutor decides if they want to file formal charges for that crime, tack on additional charges, or drop the case completely. The prosecutor will investigate to determine the correct statute needed to issue specific charges in that particular state, and examine the evidence: physical evidence, videotapes, witness interviews, etc. It is important to remember that in the state of Florida, you are not permitted to take depositions in misdemeanor cases without prior approval from the judge.

Next are the "depositions," or formal meetings with very strict rules that must be followed. At a deposition, your defense attorney can sit down with the witnesses and a court reporter, asking questions about their potential statements while under oath at trial. During this discovery process, your defense attorney will also reach out to the prosecutor and begin negotiations on your behalf, if that's what you want him to do. He may begin moving toward a plea bargain in the case. If a valid defense can be shown (such as self-defense), your attorney will work to convince the prosecution that the state should drop the case.

After this middle ground of discovery takes place, the trial period begins. You'll be required to be with your attorney in court. Including jury selection, and depending on the charges, a jury trial can last anywhere from one day to several weeks. Having said that, understand that a large percentage of cases are resolved before going to trial. Usually, resolution takes place during the discovery phase of the case before trial. Your criminal defense attorney will give you very good advice on whether you should accept the prosecution's offer and plead to the case, or plead not guilty and attempt to get the case dismissed through a jury trial.

Deciding between a plea or a trial is one of the most important reasons why you'll need the expert help of your attorney. Of course, the final decision is yours as the client. However, an experienced lawyer can give very good advice on whether or not the plea is a good deal for you as the accused, or if it's a bad deal, and you should take the case in front of a jury of your peers. The lawyer will look at the case as a whole, after which you'll consult with him about the particulars: the physical evidence, potential help or harm regarding the evidence, witness testimony, potential topics on direct examination, potential cross-examination topics that might work in your favor, etc.

Based on experience, your criminal defense attorney can also offer guidance on the judges in that jurisdiction. The attorney will know how they tend to rule in cases, whether they move forward to a trial, and the kind of sentence you might get if you lose the trial. Truly, the plea-or-trial decision is really why you hire your counselor; it's where they can really help by telling you the pros and cons of each decision.

EXERCISE YOUR FIFTH AMENDMENT RIGHTS

Let's assume you've hired your attorney, or have otherwise "lawyered up." One of the most important things that clients need to know—long before they're ever arrested—is that volunteering information to the police is almost never a good idea.

This happens all too often during an arrest by the police. The suspect is read his Miranda rights and is given a choice about whether or not to speak to the police. His first instinct—most often when he knows that he is innocent—is to give the police his side of the story. As citizens, we train our children to be polite and helpful. They want to be honest and to communicate or defend themselves at that point. As a criminal defense attorney, I caution people that *they should not do this*! Most often, no matter what your instincts or your emotions tell you, saying nothing is the best policy. Stay calm, listen to your Miranda Rights, and remain silent. When you're speaking to law enforcement, all you're doing is giving additional evidence to the police. You have your Fifth Amendment right to remain silent. At this point, exercise it.

If you think that you are innocent of the crime for which you've been arrested, it's still best to exercise your constitutional right to remain silent. When you hire an attorney, you can and should have an open conversation with that attorney about the sequence of events when you were arrested; in turn, your attorney can explain your side of the story to the police officer or the prosecution. *Under no circumstances is it a good idea to give information or your side of the story at the time of arrest.* If your mother was like mine, she probably always told you "honesty is the best policy." That's still true in many settings, but when you're dealing with our criminal justice system or asked questions right after you're arrested, it's best to just to remain silent and speak with an attorney as soon as possible.

Of course, during a trial, honesty is the best policy when you're under oath. You're not allowed to be untruthful to the jury or the judge. When you're first arrested, though, do your best to remain calm, ask for an attorney, and then speak honestly with that attorney. Let your paid criminal defense lawyer communicate your opinions and your defenses to the prosecution at a later time.

YOU AND MIRANDA

Along those same lines, if you are like most people, you may not fully understand the Miranda warnings. Sometimes, they labor under the incorrect assumption that because they were not read their Miranda warnings, the case can or will be thrown out of court. In order for the police to read your Miranda warnings, two things must be true:

- You must be in police custody. This means you're not free to leave, you're handcuffed, you're in the back of a police car, or you're in jail.

- You are being interrogated by the police. Interrogation means that they are asking you questions and looking for answers about what led to your arrest.

This does not mean that the case will be automatically thrown out. If the police fail to Mirandize you correctly, then anything that you say after the Miranda warnings, any admissions that you make, will not be able to be used against you in court. However, your case will not be dismissed because of this omission alone.

If you are in police custody and are being questioned by the police, it's best to be polite, be courteous, ask for an attorney, and not volunteer anything. As a former prosecutor, I can tell you that the best weapon in a prosecutor's arsenal is an admission by the accused. Just as the Miranda warning states, they can and probably will use that admission in a jury trial. If you confess to the crime, it's going to make your attorney's job a lot harder in the future.

STAND YOUR GROUND

Recently, there have been some very high profile cases, and more than a little debate about Florida's "stand your ground" statute. It is related to self-defense. Without getting into too many specifics of the law, self-defense is one of the most critical defenses available to a criminal defense attorney. It's necessary to carefully examine cases of aggravated battery or any other violent crime; many times, after an attorney speaks to the clients who are charged with striking someone, it becomes clear that the real reason for their actions was a fear of the other person. Many times, clients were in fear for their lives, and they needed to protect themselves. This can be a valid self-defense argument.

It doesn't always happen that the person called a "victim" by the state is acting with the best intentions. A defense attorney should always look carefully into any case involving violence or an act of violence, and see if there's another reason why their client is getting charged with this violent act. Many times, it's because the accused person was trying to protect himself, another person, or his property. The law has very specific and detailed self-defenses available if that applies to the situation. Frequently, after an attorney has begun investigating or talking to the witnesses, it will be possible to get the state attorney or the prosecutor to either reduce or drop the charges altogether because the accused was simply defending himself. It's always possible that law enforcement was given insufficient or incorrect information at the scene of the crime.

PRE-TRIAL MOTIONS

"Pre-trial motions" is a general term for any motion filed before your trial date. The most common type of pre-trial motion is called a "motion to suppress." Motions to suppress are often filed in drug or narcotics cases; the attorney asserts that the police-seized evidence was seized in an unconstitutional manner; therefore, that evidence should be thrown out, along with the entire case. A very common situation would include someone stopped after driving in an automobile for a particular reason. In many recent cases, people have been stopped for a traffic citation, running a stop sign, running a red light, or experiencing a problem with their car. The police, for whatever reason, feel that they have probable cause to search their automobile; in some instances, they find some sort of contraband drugs in their car.

SELECTING A JURY

While bench trials do happen in smaller criminal cases (such as criminal traffic cases), when you want to move along the cases very quickly, in my experience it's almost always more favorable to have a jury trial in criminal cases. You're going to want to exercise your constitutional right to a trial by jury; in Florida, this will typically consist of six people for almost all non-capital criminal offenses. In Florida, criminal bench trials are rare.

After practicing law for just under ten years, I've done a number of trials as a prosecutor and as a criminal defense attorney. I really think that jury selection is probably the most important part of any trial. Many lawyers do jury selection by asking potential jurors a lot of questions, basically getting them to say yes or no to different questions like this: "Can you be impartial or can you be fair in this case?"

It can become similar to cross-examination in that the jurors really only give one-word or two-word responses to the questions. In my experience, it's a more effective jury selection method to open up communication with potential jurors by asking about their background, by getting them to openly talk about their feelings regarding the criminal law and our justice system.

Much of it depends upon the case. For example, if the case revolves around a marijuana charge, the attorney would want them to explain and open up about their opinions on marijuana use in the United States. Do they think it should be legal? Are they in favor of medical marijuana? Are the current laws effective by way of regulation? Did they ever use marijuana in college? Did they ever inhale? It's good to get them talking on their own.

As a younger lawyer, I believe that I made a mistake in doing all of the talking myself rather than letting potential jurors speak about their own feelings and getting them to talk. That is a better way to learn more about them without having cross-examination conversations with the potential jurors. I think that it's the most important part of the trial. As a lawyer, you want to know a little bit more about their background; in my experience, people from different backgrounds are going to see facts on a case differently than others.

WITNESSES

A criminal defense attorney does have the right to call witnesses in a case and present his client's case to the jury; however, many defense attorneys don't want to call a large list of their own witnesses and pit their statements against the prosecution's witnesses. Generally, most of the criminal defense attorney's job is cross-examining witnesses put on by the prosecution. Mostly, the prosecutor will be doing "direct examination"; they'll be taking the witness through what they saw or what they know about the case. Then the defense attorney will cross-examine those same witnesses. During a cross-examination, the defense attorney wants to focus on whether or not the witness has a potential agenda or was given any specific benefit: any potential bias, any favorable treatment by the prosecution, or any favorable pre-deal by the prosecution for their testimony. The defense attorney will also ask whether or not the witnesses were ever under investigation and then given favorable treatment, or if they are enjoying any profit as a result of their given testimony.

During cross-examination, the attorney will also want to find out any inconsistencies, such as the witness changing his story in any way. Perhaps he gave a statement to the police at the time of the arrest that is inconsistent with either the deposition or his trial testimonies. Many times, during cross-examination, the poor memory of the witness can be revealed by way of these inconsistent or false statements given in the past. Next, it's also necessary to examine whether or not this witness had the ability to see if the accused might have been impaired or intoxicated at the time of the arrest. Was the view of the witness obstructed at any point? Is the witness a friend or a relative of the victim in the case? Those are a few of the things that come to mind in terms of witness examination.

CLOSING ARGUMENTS

Ultimately, when the attorney has finished with the witnesses, he will have to summarize everything for the jury. The closing argument is always a very vital part of the trial. Lawyers debate about whether opening or closing is the more important of the two arguments. Many lawyers take the position that the opening is more important, because studies show that people make up their minds early on in the case. Even before they know the facts, even before they hear the evidence (and even though they're not supposed to), they've subconsciously made a determination about the guilt or innocence of the accused. The closing argument is for the jurors who are not yet convinced either way—

the ones who have not yet made up their minds. For them, a powerful closing argument can make all the difference.

I think that members of a jury generally remember what's been said, what hasn't been said, or how people reacted to things. In a closing argument, I try to really connect the dots from cross-examination. Rather than just rehashing the facts and the testimonies, which is what I used to do, now I attempt tell the jury why those facts and testimonies matter. For example, I'll spend time telling them that the witness testified about a red car but it was really gray, and why that matters to the case the state presented. Instead of arguing with the witness at the time of cross-examination, or just writing down that fact and bringing out that testimony in cross-examination, I bring it up at the closing argument instead. I review it and ask the jury why that mattered, or indicate why that inconsistency makes the accused innocent, or note how that particular fact means that the state did not prove their case beyond a reasonable doubt.

The way that many judges operate, defense attorneys usually have just a few minutes to look over their notes and give a very important closing argument. For my own cases, I try to back-track and talk about some of the topics that were covered during jury selection. For instance, I remind the jury that they all agreed that even though the defendant hadn't testified, they may not hold that against him. If we talked in jury selection about the fact that jurors must put away their biases, I remind them to be fair and partial. Then I review the points that were made on cross-examination of the first witness, the points that were made on cross-examination of the second witness, and so forth. Then I talk about what the prosecutor told the jury that he was going to prove at the beginning of the case, and why he failed to prove that after all. Presenting a chronological story is a very good way to organize a final argument. It's more effective to review not only what the witnesses said but also why those facts are important as you go along.

THE KEY TO A GOOD DEFENSE

In defending somebody against criminal charges, many things matter and can make for a good result at a trial. In my opinion, the earlier that you can hire a criminal defense attorney, the better off you'll be. If the attorney is hired early on, he or she can (if necessary) provide the prosecutor with really critical information that maybe helpful to everyone concerned. I see many people who have been charged with possession of a controlled substance or another drug-related charge. Maybe they were going to the doctor's office, and for whatever reason, they were carrying pills around in their pocket when they were arrested. It frequently turns out later that the accused actually did have a prescription for the drugs. At that point, the defense attorney can simply provide the prescription information to the prosecutor and get the case dropped.

People sometimes wonder about an "alibi defense." An alibi would mean that you weren't the person who committed the crime—it was another person's fault. By raising the alibi defense, you'd have to have a witness come in and testify that you were at a different location with that witness at the time that the offense occurred. Essentially, "it wasn't me, I couldn't have done the crime; I was with my alibi witness somewhere else." This defense is fairly rare. Most of the cases that I deal with involve self-defense or another form of defense.

The self-defense argument is a good one. The prosecutor may only be seeing facts presented by law enforcement at the time.

There may be a valid self-defense argument that is unknown by the prosecution, and the defense attorney can provide them with pertinent background information. Sometimes, background information about the events and circumstances of the crime can be one-sided—the police may have primarily received information from the victim and his friends. When the prosecution is informed about the other side of the story or is given additional witness statements, he may decide that this case is not something he wants to pursue, and simply drops the case.

In Florida, the prosecution has the ability to drop the case after arrest but before formal charges are filed. Getting an attorney involved at an early stage can really help. The defense attorney may show the prosecutor some additional mitigating information that can move the charge down to a misdemeanor and remove possible prison time, or even reduce the consequences to just a fine. Getting the whole story in front of the prosecutor is key.

(This content should be used for informational purposes only. It does not create an attorney-client relationship with any reader and should not be construed as legal advice. If you need legal advice, please contact an attorney in your community who can assess the specifics of your situation.)

[1] http://www.masshist.org/publications/apde2/view?id=ADMS-05-03-02-0001-0004-0016

9

MISCARRIAGE OF JUSTICE — WHEN THE SYSTEM MAKES A WRONG TURN

by David S. Mejia, Esq.

David S. Mejia, Esq.
David S. Mejia, Attorney at Law
Louisville, Kentucky
www.louisville-criminal-defense-attorney.com

David Mejia graduated from the University of Illinois at Chicago where he majored in Criminal Justice Administration with a Bachelor of Arts degree in 1973. He went on to earn his law degree from Loyola University of Chicago School of Law in 1976. He practices from his main office in Louisville, Kentucky. He also maintains an active practice in Chicago, Illinois.

Attorney Mejia has over 30 years of trial and appellate experience in the federal and state courts of Illinois and Kentucky. He concentrates in criminal defense, federal criminal defense, defense of capital murder, income tax prosecutions, as well as the litigation of habeas corpus and post-conviction petitions. He has successfully defended individuals charged with conspiracy racketeering, white collar crimes, fraud and corruption, murder, narcotic trafficking, pornography and sex crimes prosecutions.

Attorney Mejia's reputation is that of a tireless fighter for the rights of his clients. He is also well respected among his peers. He has been consistently recognized by his peers for excellence in both legal ability and professional ethics.

MISCARRIAGE OF JUSTICE—WHEN THE SYSTEM MAKES A WRONG TURN

"The strong light of the apartment left no doubt of his identity," wrote Sir Walter Scott in his historical novel, *Guy Mannering or The Astrologer* (1815). If only - in our criminal justice system of trials and verdicts - identifications were so permanently error-free. Over the past century, despite Scott's account of an unassailably true identification, irreparable misidentification that leads to the wrongful conviction of those who are innocent is appallingly recurrent in criminal courts across the country. It starts with the way investigations proceed. The routine course of a criminal investigation, more or less, goes this way: the police receive a report of a crime and then they conduct an interview of a witness, a victim, or a person with information in an effort to get a description of the assailant or suspect. In many cases, this is where the seed of misidentification is planted. Crimes such as a violent attack, assault, or robbery in the street or a home are virtually always committed by one who is a stranger to the victim.

As police embark on a search to locate this unknown individual, they use a database of prior offenders. They begin with the general description provided by the victim, which nearly always includes the suspect's height, weight, and approximate age. A "line-up" or photo spread is the first—and unfortunately too often the last—investigation tool used by law enforcement seeking to identify the perpetrator of a crime. This can (and too often does) result in the arrest and prosecution of the wrong person. Individuals who have a prior record of a conviction for a similar offense are brought to the police station for a line-up. The victims *want* to help the officer solve the crime. Therefore, they can be influenced fairly easily. Through verbal or non-verbal cues or suggestions, whether done consciously or not, police can steer witnesses or victims by asking them to concentrate and look harder at one person in the line-up. The officer may say, "He's there," and, "This person has a record. We don't want to let him go this time. We want to help you. We believe this is the man, if you want to look at person number three very closely." The police officer, due to his own police bias, may have a strong or a weak hunch; but it's just that: a hunch. What, on a particular night in a police station line-up, began as a hunch—and with the passage of time, months or years later, a trial, before a jury—is transformed into a 100% positive identification. This phenomenon occurs without the jury and even the witness knowing it, but the police know it. Sometimes, so does the prosecutor.

Let's say we have a cross-racial investigation of a violent offense that took place in the darkness of night in less than minutes. The victim may say, "Well, it was an African-American male, 20s, who had a tight hairstyle. He was wearing jeans and a hoodie and he was around 5'6" to 5'11"." You can imagine how many human beings fit this description.

The entire process of achieving a reliable identification is tricky to begin with. Universities have done experiments in which an individual will race through a full classroom of students, shout, commit some shocking abrupt stunt, and then flee the classroom. All students in the room are then asked about what they observed. "Describe the person's words or conduct. Describe the person's clothing. Tell me whether the individual that you saw had glasses or not. Did he have facial hair? What was his hairstyle or hair color?" Despite the room full of students being asked to relate the above information within moments of the incident, the error rate is astonishing. A combination of shock and high emotion, coupled with a swift and unexpected display, produces a high error rate.

Similar studies, when the class is one race and the sudden intruder into the classroom is a different race, produce an even higher rate of misidentification, misinterpretation of the words of the intruder, and error in describing his conduct. So too, the error rate increases when the gender, age group, and demographics are disparate. For instance, a white person in his 60s has greater difficulty in distinguishing characteristics of Orientals in their teens. As a matter of fact, statistical studies show as we get older—into our 30s, 40s, and 50s—that it becomes increasingly difficult to differentiate between someone who is 16 years old and someone who is in his mid-twenties. To make matters even worse, when it comes to irreparable cross-racial misidentification, as people grow older, it is more difficult to differentiate between black males between the ages of 20 and 30 who have similar hairstyles, common typical facial hair, and no glasses. Of course, there is greater accuracy in distinguishing characteristics of people who share our own race, but that doesn't help if there is a cross-racial component.

When individuals view a line-up, whether they are eyewitnesses or actual crime victims, they are going through a mental process of elimination. They look at the five people, but they are not necessarily choosing the one who actually committed the crime. Instead, they are eliminating four of the five standing in the line-up who look *least* like the perpetrator. This is not the same as actually identifying the offender who committed the crime. A criminal event or incident usually occurs at night, in minutes, under stressful conditions. The witness or victim is usually in shock. Considering the very limited time frame, opportunity to observe, process, and retrieve the events that took place is extremely difficult. Then, when the victim or witness is asked to view a line-up, that person must choose the man or woman who looks most similar to the offender after having ruled out the other individuals standing with him in the police station.

Misidentification can occur in another way. When someone is accosted on the street, the trauma, fear, and sheer jolt at surviving the event itself can trigger distortion of memory. We know that individuals often see characteristics that are not actually present. What happens in the line-up is the victim sees a characteristic and adopts that characteristic as having been that of the attacker. For example, the victim may perceive his assailant to have been a really large man—"He HAD to be huge because he overcame ME!"—even though the attacker was actually of average build. Pity the last oversized man, generally fitting the description of the assailant, who the police previously arrested in that precinct or area of the city.

Identifications migrate. By that, I mean that an initial identification by the eyewitness might be less than positive by stating that the accused in custody "looks like" the one who committed the crime. Later, before the case comes to pre-trial hearing or jury trial, the police report of that identification is written up as a "100% positive identification," inconsistent with the initial, less-than-positive identification. Unfortunately, at trial, the jury only hears that the eyewitness or victim "positively identified" the defendant. Hearing that, the judge and the jury conclude, notwithstanding all that surrounded the identification process giving it doubt and unreliability, that it was positive rather than tentative. In the years that follow, the public record, discourse, and commentary on such cases becomes, "How could he have been 'positively' identified at trial when DNA evidence established the guilt of another and six defense witnesses all testified he could not have committed the crime for the reason that he was with friends and family at the time of the crime?"

Unfortunately, too many lawyers do not have the knowledge, skill, and ability to challenge an in-court identification or to demonstrate that the accused himself is a victim of an irreparable misidentification and is actually innocent. Far too many lawyers lack the professional training and experience to conduct a thorough enough investigation of the police investigative process or to locate and produce convincing evidence for a jury that someone can actually be wrong in identifying the accused. This unfortunate condition in my profession leads to far too many plea bargains for innocent defendants in order to avoid larger prison sentences.

With the high number of misidentifications, and data showing its frequency, national standards have been suggested and put in place in some states, which seek to control police abuse in the way photo and line-up identifications are conducted. For example, the detective or officer who interviews the crime victim or witness should not be allowed to participate in the line-up or photo spread procedure. The police officer arranging for the line-up, selecting its participants, and perhaps having awareness of the suspect, likewise, should have no contact with the eyewitness or victim viewing the line-up. Of course, the five or six individuals placed in the line-up, or selected for the photo spread, should be similar in height, facial characteristics, and clothing. Keep in mind, the officer or officers who place the non-suspects *know* they didn't commit the crime for the simple reason that they have been in custody or locked up and, therefore, could not have committed the crime. Thus, the police officer's hunch that the actual suspect is the perpetrator of the offense can easily and wrongly steer the person viewing the line-up toward that individual.

THE REMEDY

All states have provisions that can come into play when there is newly discovered evidence. When this happens, an individual convicted and imprisoned can petition to return to court by applying for what is called "post-conviction relief." He must show that newly discovered evidence has surfaced which was not available or known at trial. It must also show that the defendant could not have known about the evidence and was unaware of its existence during his trial. It is through subsequent investigation by a new attorney or a witness or someone coming forward that the new evidence is provided. It is evidence of such a character that, had the prosecution and defense known of it and presented it at trial, it would have changed the outcome of the case. Post-conviction petitions attack the integrity of the verdict. What is essentially being said is that had this evidence been made available at the time of the trial and had the evidence been presented to a jury, the result would have been different. The defendant may very well have been found not guilty.

In some cases, a convicted individual may seek post-conviction relief saying, "I've now heard, read and investigated, and thoroughly reviewed my case, and I see that my lawyer was professionally inadequate. My lawyer didn't investigate properly. My lawyer didn't prepare. My lawyer was negligent in failing to interview me thoroughly. He failed to go to the scene and examine the evidence. He failed to test and question the law enforcement officers. He told me he was a former prosecutor. He told me he was a defense lawyer. I came to find out he's primarily an accident lawyer. He's a divorce attorney. He's a personal injury attorney. I didn't have an experienced criminal lawyer. So, now, I have a skilled criminal defense attorney that has reviewed my entire trial, examined all the steps taken by my previous lawyer, and essentially has concluded that no reasonable attorney would have defended my case in the manner that mine did. Therefore, I want a hearing to determine whether my lawyer was deficient."

Essentially, this is a process that requires affirmative answers to two questions. First, was my lawyer's performance "below an objective standard of reasonableness?" Second, did my lawyer's "deficient performance result in an unreliable or fundamentally unfair outcome" in my case?

This is not an appeal but a post-conviction attack on the integrity of the process and the reliability of the verdict. This is another way by which individuals who are innocent or who have been represented by inadequate, unreasonable counsel are able to return to their trial court seeking to overturn their convictions or sentences as unconstitutional, unfair, or because of an unfair process that resulted in an innocent person being convicted of a crime he did not commit.

Different from a post-conviction petition is the right of appeal. Each person who has been convicted and sentenced in a criminal court has the automatic right to a direct appeal. That right must be exercised by filing a formal document, called a notice of appeal, normally within 30 days of the final court order convicting and sentencing him. If the notice of appeal is not filed, the federal system allows one year to take steps to question or attack the appeal based upon some error that can be described as unconstitutional. In Illinois or Kentucky, where I practice, it is relaxed and lengthened based upon what it is you are bringing to the court's attention. In Kentucky, you have three years from the date of conviction of sentence to bring the case back into court. After three years, there is another provision that allows you to bring the case back into court, but it becomes narrower and narrower as time goes by.

The law wants to rely upon, believe in, and conclude criminal cases correctly and efficiently, so the legislatures and courts have enacted a series of timeframes in which you can bring a case back to court. The law essentially says that in order to convict, there must be proof beyond a reasonable doubt. Obviously, in the cases we hear about involving newly discovered evidence, particularly in the area of scientific proof such as DNA, this evidence may not have existed 30 or 40 years ago, but it has now been discovered. It can be presented in a court of law to give truth to what the facts are and show that the conviction was wrong.

The law also says that the testimony of one person is sufficient to bring the charge. If the testimony of a single witness is consistent, reliable, and unimpeached, that is enough to prove guilt beyond a reasonable doubt. Clearly, experience shows that crime scene evidence, physical evidence such as fingerprints, hair samples, saliva, and bodily fluids, give clear proof of facts and evidence when compared to a single eyewitness' testimony.

However, in some cases we do not have physical evidence, such as in sex crimes. It then becomes a "he said, she said" prosecution and the jury is left to determine whom they believe—the accused or the victim. Through history, we know that some victims who report sexual crimes and provide testimony as to the allegation of a sexual attack or sexual misconduct later contact the authorities and say, "I lied. I didn't tell the truth. I made it up. I was motivated to say something that wasn't so. I did it because of whatever reason that was in me." Sometimes they say, "I lied because I was forced by my family or I was pressured by the police." Then, you have a very difficult case in which someone has recanted his or her testimony and where the law is then required to review the case and withdraw the allegation and sworn testimony that formed the basis of the conviction of an innocent suspect.

SAFEGUARDING YOUR INALIENABLE RIGHTS

The constitution and laws of this country are unique in the world. Our founding fathers adopted laws that provide enormous individual protection of civil liberties and rights to all people who are in America, even those who are not citizens. When initially encountered by police, an individual is permitted to ask questions such as, "Am I under arrest? Am I under investigation? Are you asking me questions as a witness or am I a suspect?"

The most important thing to know is that everyone has the right to refuse to answer questions of an officer before, during, or after arrest. Everyone has the absolute right to insist on seeing and talking to a lawyer before questioning, whether that questioning is before, during, or after arrest. These are constitutional rights that the police have sworn to uphold and respect. When individuals are pulled over or the police come to their homes, they have the right to say to police, "I'm not consenting to any entry or search of my car," and, "I do not give consent to your entry and search of my home."

When this occurs, the police must obey the motorist's or homeowner's directive regarding any search. The police absolutely must respect the individual's constitutional protections. What is commonly known as the Miranda warning, including an individual's right to silence and being informed that anything he says can and will be used against him in a court of law, is a 100-percent protection that the police must follow. If an officer approaches an individual at home and says, "I'm here to see you and to talk to you. It's important that I enter and it's important that I ask you some questions," the person must invoke his rights because if he submits to questioning by authorities without invoking those rights—what we call passive acquiescence—it is a waiver of his rights.

What commonly happens is the police have a report that a particular individual is engaged in a criminal act or is engaged in ongoing criminal conduct. The police will locate and seek to question that individual, who at this point is unaware he is a suspect. The police approach the individual without informing him that he (or she) is a suspect and actively withhold knowledge that he is under investigation. The officer simply says, "We want to talk to you." The individual talks to the officer and answers questions, all of which can be used against him to incriminate him. After answering the questions the individual will then complain, "Wait a minute! I wasn't told my rights."

According to our law, *an officer does not have an obligation to inform an individual of his right to silence and his right to counsel until after a formal arrest has been made.* Obviously, then, police approach individuals, ask them questions, obtain incriminating responses, and *then* take them into custody. At that point, they do not need to give Miranda warnings because they have already gotten the incriminating responses they seek. Nonetheless, having now been arrested, it is strongly urged that this individual *still* invoke the right to counsel and the right to silence.

No one, even those who are wrongly arrested, has the right to resist arrest. Clearly, someone who has committed an offense or knows he is under investigation for violating the law, even one who is entirely innocent, cannot flee, resist arrest, or challenge police officers in the performance of their duty. Police officers are not allowed to enter homes or residences without a warrant, the person's consent, or an emergency or exigent situation. Even if an officer violates these constitutional protections, individuals do not have the right to resist, challenge, or confront the officer in the illegal performance of his job in any way.

People need to understand this better. It's at the very center of the case in Ferguson, Missouri, of the shooting death of Michael Brown and in the Staten Island, New York, case of the police strangling death of Eric Garner. Both of these men resisted arrest. Both died, but by resisting arrest, they were each in the process of not following the instructions of uniformed officers of the law. That's illegal in and of itself.

Therefore, the rule that all of us must follow is that we must respectfully obey what police say. If police block the road, we must stop our car. If police stop us on the street, we must halt. When police confront us on the street, in the airport, or at a checkpoint and ask for identification or ask questions about where we are going and what we are doing, common notions of civic responsibility compel us to assist and cooperate with law enforcement. That being said, when police engage in illegal conduct, misconduct, or abuse, *we are not allowed to fight them.* We are not allowed to defend ourselves against such police force with force of our own. For far too long, police have engaged in illegal conduct against African-Americans and Hispanics. So, what are these groups of people to do? Well, the remedy is to surrender to that illegal authority and then take your case to court to seek redress, not resist or fight the police in the street.

Therein lies the problem. Are police permitted to use deadly force against a citizen? No. Are police allowed to use deadly force against a citizen who runs, resists arrest, or poses a danger to them? They absolutely are. Police find themselves in this situation all the time. Again, we are confronting this problem in several cases in the national news today.

If there is police misconduct, we need the assistance of other citizens who witnessed the police misconduct to come forward to give witness to what occurred. Obviously, no one can know with absolute certainty what happened in the Ferguson case and no one can know what happened in other cases, but I advise clients in every instance, it is improper, it is illegal, and it is a crime to resist police arrest—even an illegal police arrest.

First, I think we need to recognize that there are differences among us. There are differences between cultures and societies: people of different color, people of different race. You may view some as strange or different. In our history, particularly in this country, there are certain biases and prejudices that exist within our minds and our hearts. Sadly, these spring from no other source other than the color of one's skin, the style or texture of one's hair, the tone or accent of another's voice. We have to recognize that we all withdraw a little into ourselves when we are confronted with someone who is of a different race, ethnicity, or culture. Why is that? It may be some protective instinct left over from the days of our ancient ancestors. When we recognize this, I think we consciously understand that these things really do exist no matter how "unenlightened" such a reaction might be.

What do we know about how the criminal justice system works with respect to race? Decades-long national crime statistics and studies showing arrest rates for every state are kept and published. As recently as the past five years, with respect to African-American youth, compiled police records demonstrate that, while they make up 17% of the youth population, they are just under 30% of all drug-related arrests and almost 50% of all youth detained (jailed) for drug offenses. This means black youths are arrested at twice the rate of white youths, despite statistics showing near-equal drug use by black and white youths alike. In arrests for weapons and aggravated assaults, African-American youths are, in the case of weapons, arrested at twice the rate of white youth and in the area of aggravated assault, three times the rate of white youth. This is racial disparity. It is seen in juvenile arrests, imprisonment, and prosecutions as a whole.

The government statistics call this unequal enforcement of the law the "race effect" because at some stage of the juvenile justice process, the outcome of the case for minorities is for the worse. Marijuana alone, just its possession for personal use, is enforced unequally in this country. Statistics show that African-Americans are four times more likely to be arrested by the police for mere possession of marijuana. To me, this is institutional racism. It should not be ignored. I think the reaction of the African-American community to the several recent incidents in Missouri, Staten Island, and Cleveland reflect that blacks in this country know and feel what has been taking place and, in their way, decry it.

These are astounding statistics to confront. These numbers are such that African-Americans can rightly say they are not being treated equally. How is it that a police officer can make a decision to consistently arrest in greater proportions African-Americans and Hispanics? It has to be the color of the skin. It cannot be anything else because that is how we distinguish one person from another. Do they have the right to complain and challenge? You better believe they do. I believe they do and they should. But it needs to be done peaceably—according to the law, through legal remedies in the courts and in the state legislatures.

As a criminal lawyer, I deal with unlawful conduct by police against my clients. I'm strengthened and inspired by Justice Louis Brandeis who, in his famous dissenting opinion in the *Olmstead* case, addressing citizens' right to privacy and freedom from wrongful police intrusion, wrote these words:

> *"Decency, security and liberty alike demand that government officials shall be subjected to the same rules of conduct that are commands to the citizen. In a government of laws, existence of the government will be imperiled if it fails to observe the law scrupulously. Our Government is the potent, the omnipresent teacher. For good or for ill, it teaches the whole people by its example. Crime is contagious. If the Government becomes a lawbreaker, it breeds contempt for law; it invites every man to become a law unto himself; it invites anarchy. To declare that, in the administration of the criminal law, the end justifies the means - to declare that the Government*

may commit crimes in order to secure the conviction of a private criminal - would bring terrible retribution. Against that pernicious doctrine this Court should resolutely set its face." (Olmstead v. United States, 277 U.S. 438, at page 485 (1928))

THE TERRIBLE COST OF NOT DEFENDING YOURSELF

The initial court appearance of an accused is important. There are many things to address, such as the decision to plead not guilty or enter a plea bargain. When one goes to court and says two words, "Not guilty," this triggers a number of very important and precious constitutional protections. It triggers your right to a trial. It triggers your right to see and confront all of the evidence against you. It triggers the right to a determination of your guilt or innocence. It triggers the obligation of the prosecution to prove your guilt beyond reasonable doubt. It triggers your right to remain silent or to testify. It triggers your right to call witnesses in your defense. It triggers your right to argue for innocence and your right, if convicted and sentenced, to appeal.

If you go to court and say, "I want a plea bargain. I want a reduced charge," all of those rights are gone, swept away by your decision. All of those rights I just listed are called "waived." All are gone forever. When you plead guilty, you are permanently a convicted felon or misdemeanant. What does that do? Well, it can have both direct and collateral consequences in terms of licensing. You may not be able to be a real estate agent. You may not be able to be a doctor or a lawyer. It means you will never work in state or federal government. You may have many fewer employment opportunities. It could affect your financial life and your ability to get a loan. It may increase your likelihood of being stopped by police in the future because police will automatically think, "Oh, this is a person who's been to court and has been convicted."

Therefore, the decision to negotiate a plea bargain relinquishes numerous enormous opportunities and rights—most importantly, your right to require the state or government to prove its case against you. When confronted with criminal prosecution, I think people do a couple of things that they should not do. They call a lawyer and say, "Well how much will it cost for you to be my attorney?" Instead, they should be asking a lawyer, "I've been charged with this offense. What does it mean? What does it mean if I'm convicted?" It isn't just, "Will I go to jail?" Too many people say things like, "I've been charged with writing bad checks. I've been charged with stealing from my former employer. I've been charged with entering someone's property illegally. I've been charged with a DUI. I've been charged with making false statements or deception." The consequence of not adding these four words, "and I'm not guilty," is enormous.

FINDING THE RIGHT ATTORNEY

Let's assume a person has been arrested and is waiting to go to court the next morning. He must now realize, if he didn't before, that the police have concluded or believe he committed a crime. Assume, too, that he is on probation or parole and is mindful of the fact that if he is returned to court, his parole and probation will be revoked. He could face the consequences of imprisonment. So, he is searching for an attorney. The two important questions to any prospective attorney must be, "Are you a lawyer who has handled cases like mine?" and, "How many and with what results?" If you do not have a lawyer with experience in cases like yours, you have the wrong attorney. Follow-up questions should include, "Can you tell me what the possible results are for a case like mine?" and, "Can you tell me what your success rate is in my kind of case?" One of the least important questions to ask an attorney is whether he/she has ever been a prosecutor for the city, state, or county.

Choosing a defense lawyer on the single basis that he or she was a prosecutor is not a prudent decision. Most former prosecutors took that job right out of law school, held it for a couple of years, and then went into private practice. It takes years and years of experience, skill, evidence hearings, and jury trials defending prosecuted individuals to be a good criminal defense lawyer. There are former prosecutors who become splendid criminal defense lawyers, but if you hire an attorney just because he or she was a former prosecutor, thinking there is some special advantage by virtue of that, this logic or thinking is flawed.

The question of what the attorney charges for his services is something that you do need to know, because no one that I have encountered in my 30 years of doing this had an amount of money set aside in a bank account, in their home, or anywhere else just in case he or she was ever arrested and faced criminal prosecution. I've never met a client who was financially or (at first) emotionally prepared for confronting the criminal justice system. When facing a criminal charge, you must realistically assess what is at stake: "If I am convicted, will I go to prison? Could I lose my job? If I am convicted, will I lose opportunities in the future?"

Once you have determined that this is a skilled and experienced criminal defense attorney, meet with that lawyer to have a candid, honest, private, and privileged conversation to tell him, "This is who I am. This is my family, my life, my home, my work, and my education. This is what I'm charged with. What are going to be the results or consequences if I'm convicted? How is it going to impact me?" The one thing I do with an individual is say, "Well, let me ask you this. How much do you make a year? Give me a yearly income. Just ballpark, an average." Remember, even after an initial consultation, and later, an accused always retains the right to choose a different lawyer if the relationship becomes uncomfortable, strained, or unproductive.

A good criminal lawyer would say, "Let's look at the offense for which you're being prosecuted. If you're convicted, you will face six months to four years in jail, so you do the math. If you earn $25,000 a year, then that is $100,000 you could potentially lose if you are convicted. What is at stake is $100,000, to say nothing of the collateral consequences. Now, here is my fee." Most reasonable, experienced criminal defense lawyers will charge anywhere from $150 or $300 per hour up to $500 an hour or more, depending on the attorney. Ask the lawyer, "How many hours will it require to defend me in this case? How much work will be involved? What would the investigation be? How much is it going to cost for out-of-pocket expenses?" The normal defense for a felony, depending on the area of the country where you live, can be as little as $5,000 up to $25,000. A complex, difficult case might be $30,000 or more.

Even a large amount of money such as $25,000 is less than the risk you may be facing. Someone might say, "Well, I'm going to get probation. I'm not going to go to jail." Okay. If you get probation, you will have conditions of the probation that if you violate, you will go to jail for four years. The possibility is still there.

If you measure the cost of the attorney in this way, then you get a better idea as to what is at stake. Too many people simply say, "Give me the least amount that it will cost to be my attorney." Let's assume one lawyer quoted $8,000 to represent you but another attorney quoted you $1,000. If you hire the attorney who charges you $1,000, you save $7,000. Experience has taught us that if you hire a lawyer at a cut rate, you are buying a guilty plea. You are buying a lawyer who will not defend you. You are buying a lawyer who will not investigate your case. You are buying a lawyer who will not prepare a proper defense. The likely result is that you will be a permanently convicted felon. Too many times, I have individuals come into the office and say, "Mr. Mejia, I have two felony convictions. Can you help me? This is my third prosecution. And now, the stakes are enormous." What have they learned?

You must pay for a defense to a criminal charge just as you do when you go to see a doctor. You pay for medical tests, follow-up examinations, and hospital procedures. You pay large amounts of money per day for hospitalization. Why? You do it because your life is at stake. Your health and welfare are at stake. Your income is at stake. Your future is at stake. You should approach criminal prosecution and the criminal justice system in the same way. There is so much at stake if you choose not to go into court and say, "not guilty," with a capable, experienced, skilled criminal defense attorney.

The best way to find a good criminal defense attorney in your town or city is to call the first attorney's name you find, whether it is someone's lawyer, a worker's compensation attorney, or an attorney who wrote a will for someone you know. Ask that attorney one simple question. Ask, "Mr. Attorney, if you were charged with a serious offense, what lawyer in this city would you hire?" The attorneys in the community know who the seasoned, skilled criminal defense lawyers are because there are some of us who spend a good deal of our career defending other lawyers who are under investigation, who are in trouble with their license, who are facing discipline, or who are facing criminal investigation. The fundamental question to ask any lawyer is whom he would hire if he were under investigation or charged with a serious crime.

As I have said before, you go to a lawyer who is recommended to you as a good criminal defense attorney and ask him the two fundamental questions: "How many cases like mine have you handled in this office?" and, "What were the results in those cases." If the lawyer cannot answer those questions or the lawyer is put off by those questions, then you are in the wrong law office.

You would be surprised at the number of lawyers who hold themselves out as criminal defense lawyers who never go to trial. In every case they have, they seek a plea bargain. The vast majority of cases are plea bargained, and are resolved by mutual agreement of the parties. However, from the defense side, you want a lawyer who will negotiate reductions of charges to lesser offenses that do not carry the consequences or prison sentences of the charge that you are facing. But you essentially need a lawyer who goes to trial, defends cases, and wins cases when the evidence is insufficient to prove guilt beyond a reasonable doubt. You should always ask your attorney, "How many years have you been doing this?" and, "Can you tell me what's going to happen if I'm convicted?" You want an attorney with many years of experience handling criminal cases. If he has that experience, he will be able to answer the question, "What will happen, and what is the potential minimum and maximum punishment upon conviction?"

Lawyers also need to ask important questions of a client. "How's your physical health? How's your mental health? Tell me your side. Give me your whole, honest explanation of what happened here." Ultimately, a lawyer who understands the importance and necessity of all the rights I have talked about—who has investigated criminal cases, who has defended criminal cases, who has successfully defeated the state's or government's effort to prosecute and convict—is the lawyer you want to hire.

If you are facing a criminal investigation or prosecution, do not believe everything the police say or predict how easily they can and will prove you guilty and send you to prison. Don't just give up because the police are scary. Despite the immense power of police to arrest, investigate and provide testimony in criminal proceedings, *police do not decide guilt. Prosecutors do not decide guilt.* Only juries determine guilt or innocence. If, at any time, the lawyer you've hired to defend you expresses fear of police, terminate that attorney. That's how so many people end up pleading guilty and are left with a lifelong burdensome conviction weighing down on their shoulders. A good lawyer understands and knows that an allegation is not proof, that a charge is not evidence, that being arrested and even placed on trial does not mean you are automatically going to be convicted. If you have a lawyer who says to you, "Well, the police are going to say this; you have no chance of winning because it's you against the police," keep in mind that the Sixth Amendment guarantees every person accused of an offense the counsel of his choice. When a lawyer expresses this palpable fear of police, he should be politely terminated.

HOW CAN YOU DEFEND THEM WHEN YOU KNOW THEY'RE GUILTY?

I'd like to conclude with the ever-recurring question that every criminal defense lawyer, including myself, has repeatedly been asked by friends, relatives, and social acquaintances, "How can you defend those people who you know are guilty?"

What astonishes me is that I'm *not* asked, "How can you defend a person you know is innocent?" Realizing the enormous consequence of conviction, imprisonment, and all that will follow someone forever places an enormous task and responsibility on me and my office. It's challenging to overcome and ultimately defeat a prosecution team consisting of numerous law enforcement officials, police, the office of the prosecution with all their resources, and lamentably, a society that condemns those who are supposed to be presumed innocent as guilty—guilty despite the lack of evidence or proof of guilt. When I know my client is innocent I am charged with protecting and defending him or her in spite of a playing field that isn't particularly level. Somebody has to keep the criminal justice system from committing the most tragic miscarriage of justice – convicting and imprisoning an innocent person. That is what it's all about for me. And that's why I do it.

(This content should be used for informational purposes only. It does not create an attorney-client relationship with any reader and should not be construed as legal advice. If you need legal advice, please contact an attorney in your community who can assess the specifics of your situation.)

10

FEDERAL VS. STATE CRIMES

by John R. Teakell, Esq.

John R. Teakell, Esq.
Law Office of John R. Teakell
Dallas, Texas
www.teakelllaw.com

John Teakell, a widely known and well-respected Texas attorney, attended Oklahoma State University, and received his law degree from the Oklahoma City University School of Law in 1985. He has since spent years on both sides of the courtroom, having served both as an Assistant US Attorney, and Senior Trial Counsel for the U.S. Securities and Exchange Commission, before opening his own criminal defense law practice in the Dallas-Fort Worth metroplex.

Mister Teakell's practice is focused upon white-collar crimes, drug charges, violent crimes including those of sexual assault. He also defends those charged with U.S. Securities and Exchange Commission violations.

Frequently published and often quoted in the National media, Teakell has distinguished himself by representing clients in thousands of complex criminal and securities charges over the years. Lessons learned as a prosecutor are regularly brought to bear in Teakell's high profile cases and media appearances.

FEDERAL VS. STATE CRIMES

It is helpful to know some of the basic differences between Federal and State prosecutions. Criminal prosecution cases in the federal system are larger, more complex, often broader in a geographic sense and greater in significance (in terms of money, larger quantities if it is a drug case, or more significant as a whole) than if it were a state case. The state system is focused more on what we refer to as "street crime." The state has some economic crimes, but they are usually smaller in dollar amounts versus what we see in the federal system.

In the federal system, the investigation period for cases is usually much longer than in most state cases. It involves a more complex set of facts. Most federal cases involve analyzing financial and other complex records that you do not typically see in a state prosecution case. Furthermore, the investigators communicate very early in a case with the United States Attorney's Office as opposed to a state system where a detective or investigator does not contact the District Attorney's office until the investigation is complete.

The federal system is a harsher system. It has much harsher sentencing guidelines based on a point system that considers several factors. For example, in white-collar cases involving money, more points are assigned as the amount of money involved increases. Increasingly higher imprisonment recommendation ranges are imposed as the points increase. For example, in a drug case, the quantity of drugs involved drives up the points. As the quantity of drugs increases, the imprisonment recommendation range increases. The federal system does not lend itself to defendants simply negotiating with the prosecutor for probation or a reduced sentence as in most state court cases.

Large white-collar crimes and large drug or drug trafficking cases are the two most common categories for federal charges. Of course, there are also a number of other types of cases including computer fraud or computer-related cases, immigration, counterfeit goods, and public corruption.

Whether it is a white-collar case or a drug trafficking case, a common charge you see in federal court is conspiracy, although a conspiracy charge can be used in any case. Conspiracy is an agreement between two or more people to do something illegal. Even if they do not accomplish the objective of the conspiracy, as long as there is an agreement and the prosecution can prove the existence of that agreement and at least one act to attempt to further the conspiracy, the defendants may be found guilty. It is a very common charge in drug cases because you often have several people involved in the conspiracy, especially if the case involves transporting illegal drugs from a foreign country into the United States or from one part of the United States to another part.

Some of the people involved in the conspiracy are obviously more culpable than others. Some participants might have a very small part to play and that is all they are paid to do. Some people may have only a slight involvement in the illegal activity, but they are involved in a crime that is fairly significant. A person need not be involved very deeply to be guilty of conspiracy. He (or she) doesn't have to be involved in every part of the crime, as far as the number of transactions or his involvement in every phase of the scheme or conspiracy. The fact that he was involved in even a small portion tends to show the prosecution that that participation was important or somewhat important to the conspiracy as far as getting the product or collecting money or whatever. It is a favorite charge of many federal prosecutors because even though a person had a very minor role, prosecutors can still charge them and get a conviction for conspiracy. This is possible because the defendant is held responsible for the acts of his co-conspirators, even though he did not actually participate in all the components of the crime.

In a federal investigation, you typically discover there is an ongoing investigation before there is a formal charge, because a federal investigation is a much larger undertaking in comparison to a state investigation. You discover that federal agents are interviewing potential witnesses or you receive a notice from your bank that the federal agents are subpoenaing your bank account records or wire transfer records. From these things, one often learns that there is an investigation. When the United States Attorney and federal agents are winding up the investigation, they often approach the target of the investigation to see if he will talk to them in the hope of gaining admissions of guilt from the target for his participation. This is true whether or not the target is potentially facing a conspiracy charge or substantive charges for possession of a controlled substance, mail fraud, money laundering, or whatever the type of investigation.

YOUR RIGHT TO REMAIN SILENT STILL APPLIES

If you are approached by an agent or a law enforcement person, you do not have to speak to him. You can refuse to talk. You are a citizen of the United States and you have your rights just like anyone else. If you are contacted, your responses to specific questions may directly implicate you; that is, your involvement in a criminal activity may be inferred from them. I recommend people politely decline and say, "I'll have an attorney get in touch with you or the prosecutor who's involved." Ask for the nature of the inquiry and for the name of the prosecutor so your attorney can contact the correct agent and the correct prosecutor. Your attorney should contact the prosecutor's office to learn what he can and keep abreast of the investigation as it goes along. Keep in mind that the investigators are not required to give you "Miranda warnings" (right to remain silent, right to an attorney, etc.); they are not required to inform you of "your rights" or "your right to remain silent" unless: 1) you are in custody (or even detained); and 2) the officer or agent initiates questioning about the subject area under investigation.

Sometimes the United States Attorney will send a letter to the target of the investigation advising him that he is the target and inviting him to come to a grand jury hearing. Usually, that prompts the target to retain legal counsel to find out the focus of the investigation and counsel him on his legal rights regarding the investigation. Normally, the attorney will advise his client not to testify before the grand jury. At a minimum, it does open discussions with the United States Attorney. In some cases, you can arrange for an indictment (meaning formal charges or the act of formally charging) negotiation or a plea agreement. If not, at least you learn what is happening and what is coming your way.

In federal investigations, unlike a state system, you are categorized in one of three roles. The first is the "target." Being a target means you are definitely someone that the United States Attorney believes he can prove, beyond reasonable doubt, is guilty of a crime. Therefore, he is working to obtain evidence during the investigation to use in the Indictment against you. The second category is "subject." This is a person whom the United States Attorney cannot say with certainty is the target of the investigation, yet he can say this person appears to have been involved in some criminal activity or may have broken a law but the investigation does not support indictment at this time. The United States Attorney wants more evidence before he continues forward with an Indictment. This is equivalent to the term "a person of interest." The third category would be a witness. If you are not a target or the subject of an investigation, then you may be a potential witness.

PRE-INDICTMENT NEGOTIATIONS AND PROFFER AGREEMENTS

Typically, once someone learns that he is the target or subject of a federal investigation, he will retain an attorney to represent him. The defense attorney contacts the United States Attorney to confirm there is an ongoing investigation and ascertain the focus of the investigation. If the investigation is far enough along, the United States Attorney may tell the defense attorney, perhaps without showing or telling him everything, what evidence has been accumulated against the client. Keep in mind that, prior to an Indictment, the government is not obligated to provide any evidence that the prosecution can use against you and that you would need in order to defend yourself. As a defense attorney, you send them a letter of representation so they will at least verbalize some of the things they have or show you examples of some of the evidence so you can inform your client.

At that point, the United States Attorney wants to obtain cooperative agreements for the defendant so fewer people need to be indicted or fewer people need to wonder if they are going to trial. You see these kinds of agreements in movies and television—there, they call it something such as "turning state's evidence." The agreement also provides another source of information or cooperation that the United States Attorney can use if the investigation is continuing. They can use this information to gain evidence to indict other people. Sometimes, but not often, it is a general statement. It does not apply across the board. Sometimes, in pre-Indictment negotiations, there is a little more play, a little more wiggle room, so to speak, between the charge to which the person pleads guilty and the charge the U.S. Attorney would have originally sought. It could be subject to negotiation depending on how firm the evidence is that the person is offering to give to the United States Attorney.

An advantage of pre-Indictment negotiations is learning that there is an ongoing investigation against your client so you can find out if it appears to be a good case and is therefore too risky to go to trial. If so, you have an agreement case and not a trial case. You can begin cutting your losses and concentrating on the larger Indictments. Some Indictments may have mandatory minimum sentences and some may require the Department of Justice's approval to dismiss the charges.

The negotiations with the United States Attorney's office, especially once you learn about the investigation, are very important. It is always to your advantage to contact them to determine what they have against you. More importantly, if you have something which can prove that you are not involved in the activity or you were only a minor player, it can help during the investigation. A person might have been involved, but he may not be as involved or responsible for as many transactions as was originally thought by the investigators. If you know about the investigation, you can present this information to the U.S. Attorney.

It is worth trying to present this information to the United States Attorney even if you do not put an end to the investigation. You might receive a different charge. You might also change the focus of the investigation so that the sentencing guidelines are lower than what you might have been facing had they indicted you as planned. For example, in the recent past, I had a client who was a target of a government contract fraud case. An attorney for another related target and I convinced the Department of Justice there was not a government contract fraud scheme. They charged the client with a tax charge instead of contract fraud. It was a lot less exposure for the client compared to what would have happened if the much larger government contract fraud charge had been filed.

You also have proffer agreements and proffer sessions in the federal system. It is referred to sometimes as a "free talk." In other words, the target of the investigation (in pre-Indictment, the target is not a defendant) agrees to come in, open up, and truthfully answer questions. As a defense attorney, you do not want your client to do this unless he already has some type of protection in place. The proffer session is considered a plea negotiation under Rule 11 of Federal Criminal Rules of Procedure; therefore, information from the session cannot be used against you during trial, if you fail to finalize an agreement. In other words, it is an incentive for the target of the investigation to come forward and openly explain what happened.

From my perspective, a defendant should attend a proffer session only if he is in one of two situations:

- The first would be if there is clearly a good case against your client and, as his defense attorney, you want to downplay his role in the crime or clarify that the client was not as involved as government believes.

- The second would be if you are on the bubble, so to speak, and you believe you have a legitimate chance to convince the United States Attorney not to go forward with indicting or formally charging.

Again, it is an incentive for the defendant to open up and explain some things. It is an incentive for the prosecution because they can hear what the target or the defendant has to say, according to his perspective.

To put it in lay terms, cooperation is built into the federal system in the sense that, if you cooperate, you may well be rewarded with a lower sentence, or possibly no charges, or a lesser charge. In a criminal case, you can receive a reduction in your potential sentence before sentencing or after sentencing if they bring you back for a re-sentencing. Sometimes, people provide information that eventually is followed up by agents, which the U.S. Attorney uses to make a case, yet the person who provided the information has been sentenced or even imprisoned by that time. If the information was used by the United States Attorney and something comes of it, then the United States Attorney can file a sentence reduction motion to reduce the person's sentence. In a state case, however, your attorney negotiates directly with the prosecutor and the court will usually accept his recommendation. The Federal rules are different since there are sentencing guidelines in the federal system.

Cooperation is built into the federal system much more than in the state system. If you come to an agreement with the United States Attorney's Office because you provide information they can use, or if you actively work for them, you can ask for a downward departure motion, which is filed under court seal. It details the type of cooperation or level of cooperation that the defendant provided and asks the court to reduce the sentencing guideline range. For example, if you are looking at a range of 87–108 months, the United States Attorney may ask the judge to come down below 87 months. It is within the discretion of the judge.

THE GRAND JURY

The grand jury is a constitutionally required process for the probable cause phase of felonies in both state and federal courts. There is nothing magical about the process. It is simply a system or a vehicle for the prosecutor to establish probable cause. Probable cause, in itself, is essential in order to establish and justify a felony charge. Probable cause carries a low burden of proof: if a reasonable person would believe that a crime was committed based on the circumstances presented, then it constitutes probable cause. Ironically, the burden of proof in a criminal case at trial is the highest burden of proof in our judicial system—the defendant *must* be found guilty beyond a reasonable doubt. We must prove the person committed the crime beyond a reasonable doubt to convict him in a criminal case, but we only require probable cause to return an Indictment.

The federal grand jury is a one-sided hearing where the prosecutor calls witnesses and presents evidence to members of the grand jury in an attempt to prove that the government has probable cause for an Indictment. The only other person who would normally be allowed in the hearing would be the stenographer.

The hearing is on the record, but it is not a formal hearing where the defendant can attend and present evidence to contradict the prosecution's case. In the state system, the state prosecutor generally allows the defendant to testify if he chooses to do so. A defendant would only want to do this if the situation allowed him to dissuade the grand jury from an Indictment. The members of the grand jury are not deciding guilt or innocence; they are only deciding if probable cause exists for an Indictment. Their job is to determine whether or not the evidence presented by the prosecution, including hearsay evidence, is sufficient to establish probable cause to believe a crime was committed.

The same rules apply both in the federal and state system with one exception. In the state system, the state prosecutor typically gives the defendant the courtesy of making a small presentation of statements from different people, maybe statements of a witness, a polygraph exam of the target of the investigation, or whatever facts you may have to counter the government's evidence. They will not allow you to make a full-blown presentation. They will allow you to make a "packet presentation"—as it is often called—or have the defendant testify in an attempt to dissuade the grand jury from indicting. At the federal level, though, this does not happen. In fact, it is a crime to try to influence a federal grand jury. Attempts to try to dissuade the prosecution in the federal system would be presented to the United States Attorney's Office for their consideration.

There is an old saying that originated a couple hundred years ago and you still hear it today: "The grand jury can indict a ham sandwich if it wants to." Basically, it means that the grand jury is kind of a rubber stamp for the prosecutor. That is why it is so important with a state grand jury to try to get information included in packet form if you believe it could dissuade the grand jury from an Indictment. For example, in the state system, if you have some information of which the prosecution is not aware or which the prosecution did not want to present to the grand jury members, if you can provide the information to the grand jury in a packet form, then you may have a chance to dissuade the grand jury from indicting you. In a federal case, you can only present your information and/or evidence to the United States Attorney in hopes he/she will decline presenting to a grand jury in your case.

MONEY LAUNDERING

Money laundering is usually more common in the federal criminal system than in the state criminal system. Sometimes people hear about the crime but do not understand what is involved in a money laundering scheme. Money laundering is taking money obtained by illegal means, money that is tainted, and using it in legal transactions. Traditional money laundering involves trying to hide funds obtained through some sort of illegal activity by transferring the money a number of times through different accounts, using it to start a legitimate business or using it to make legitimate investments. This makes the money appear to be "clean" because the properties and assets were legally purchased. The illegality could be that the original money was obtained through drug activities, embezzlement, fraud, or illegal gambling. You often see it in federal court in white-collar cases and drug cases but not as much in state court.

People typically think of money laundering as being drug-related, although it can be used in any illegal activity. There is case law that says if you take a sack of cash that was derived from selling drugs and give it to somebody, that, in itself, constitutes money laundering. In the state system, they may use another charge instead of the actual phrase "money laundering." It may be worded as an illegal investment rather than money laundering. It is not unusual to have a case in state court that began as an arrest on a traffic stop, but a search of the vehicle reveals they have thirty, forty, or even sixty thousand dollars in cash. There is case law that developed in Texas, and I believe in a number of other places, that if there is an illegal drug present, even a very small amount, there is the presumption that the funds found in the vehicle are drug-related. Many times, people may have a significant amount of cash with them, but no drugs are found and there is no evidence of tainted money. Usually the State Trooper or the Deputy Sherriff will confiscate or seize the cash and the District Attorney's Office might agree to charge the person with money laundering or they may proceed with a forfeiture action.

FORFEITURES

The civil forfeiture of the money or assets of the accused, whether it is his vehicle, his cash, or other property, is based on criminal activities. There must be a connection between the items seized and a criminal activity. In other words, the asset was going to be used for an illegal purpose or it was obtained through tainted or illegally obtained funds. The question then becomes, "Can the prosecutor prove it?"

If the prosecutor decides that there is not sufficient evidence of illegal activities, there is no investigation to begin with, or no illegal substance in the car, and there is nothing else to indicate that the monies were obtained illegally, then they may choose to forfeit the state's claim to the asset. The case can then becomes a civil action. In a civil action, the burden of proof is a lot less. The state must still establish some connection between the illegal activity and the asset. In other words, as said earlier, it was going to be used for an illegal purpose or it was obtained through illegal purposes.

Even though there may be no evidence that the payments used to purchase the vehicle were obtained from illegal activities, if the state can prove the vehicle was used to transport persons to purchase illegal drugs or transporting illegal drugs themselves, the vehicle can be subjected to forfeiture. It is not unusual to see cash, vehicles, and real estate being forfeited in these types of situations.

There is an incentive for the state and federal government to pursue forfeiture. If a forfeited vehicle is free and clear of any liens, the government can sell the vehicle or use it. In the instance of cash, they can use the cash for governmental expenses or to fund programs. On the federal level, we see a good deal of real estate being forfeited. Usually, the U.S. Marshals take control of the property and care for it until it is sold. It becomes a larger undertaking sometimes because they must care for the property until it is liquidated.

In the federal system, the Marshal Service typically oversees securing and liquidating forfeited assets. Usually, when we have situations like that, the United States Attorney is involved. There are agencies like the FBI and the DEA who physically have control over some of the assets. It may be cash. It may be a vehicle. The Marshals may not be involved in those cases until a forfeiture order from the court dictates that they become involved. On the state side, it is usually the police department or a state agency involved with the case assisting the state prosecutor's office in taking control of the forfeited asset.

ALTERNATIVES TO INCARCERATION

In the federal system, because of the U.S. Sentencing Guidelines, imprisonment is recommended for almost every offense. If your crime is low in the guidelines, you might receive probation or a non-custody sentence such as home confinement. In the state system, it is not unusual for a person who does not have much of a criminal history to receive probation or a deferred adjudication. However, in the federal system, you must contend with sentencing guidelines.

Your attorney can ask for a downward departure motion in some unique situations. He or she can argue with a judge to have a downward departure. The judge might put certain factors on record, such as the accused did cooperate but is not receiving a downward departure from the government. There is actually a variance or a defense downward departure motion available which may be used in the same case if the judge wants to come down below the recommended range of imprisonment. He can do so for those reasons or non-cooperation factors as it is articulated on the record.

DO WE GO TO TRIAL OR ENTER A PLEA AGREEMENT?

In any case, state or federal, you and your client must consider the admissible evidence. You may have evidence on the other side that is very strong which you cannot overcome. You must weigh the evidence that the prosecution has and consider the sentence you could receive if you go to trial and are found guilty of the charge versus what the sentence may be if you enter into a plea agreement. If you will receive "X" at trial but the plea agreement you are being offered gives you substantially less than "X," you must go back to the evidence to weigh your options. If the evidence is strong, it may be in your best interest to take the plea bargain. If the evidence is weak, it may be better to go to trial.

You must decide, "Is the evidence against me really that good?" and "Is it too risky to go to trial?" On the other hand, you may be asking yourself, "There is some evidence but it's not really that strong for the state or the government. Am I better off going to trial?" The question then becomes about risk. In other words, what is the risk that the evidence is good enough that the jury will find you guilty? Those are the basic factors that you look at to decide whether or not to go to trial or, in the alternative, to plead guilty.

SENTENCING GUIDELINES

In the state system, you can negotiate for probation or a minimum sentence. To do that, you negotiate directly with the prosecutor. In the federal system, you have sentencing guidelines that control sentencing or have a tremendous influence on sentencing. If the mandatory sentencing guideline for your crime is 121–151 months of imprisonment, that is quite possibly the sentence you will receive if you are found guilty. A few years ago, the Supreme Court stated that the sentencing guidelines are not mandatory but they are advisory. This ruling gives the defense attorney the argument that the sentence can be lower than the guidelines. Judges have the discretion to lower the sentences according to the ruling.

Mandatory minimum sentences are probably more prevalent in the federal system. In the state system, you might have a mandatory minimum of 15 years for a felony if you have a previous felony. However, in the federal system, there area number of mandatory minimums even if you have no criminal history. Most federal drug cases are ten years to life if found guilty. If they are not ten years to life, they are five years to 40 years. Certain sexually-related crimes have a mandatory minimum of 15 years.

The federal sentencing guidelines are found in the United States Sentencing Guidelines Manual, which was created during the 1980s. Prior to sentencing guidelines, the sentences were left to the discretion of the judge. Now, judges use the guidelines to decide whether you will be sentenced in accordance with the guidelines or if the judge will grant a lower sentence.

Another difference between the federal guidelines and the state system is the application of those guidelines. You have a pre-sentence report in federal cases that is different from the pre-sentence report in state cases. With a state case, it is mostly background information. However, the federal pre-sentence report contains the draft or proposed application of the guidelines. In other words, if it is a drug case and the quantity of drugs involved is "X," you get so many points because of the quantity of drugs involved. There are also "enhancements" that further add points. If you are an organization leader, you get points for this as well. If weapons were used, you get points added. Then you calculate those points. You may disagree with the number of points assigned to your crimes. If you disagree with the addition of enhancement points, then you can object to the guideline application.

In other words, if you disagree with the sentence, even if you plead guilty, then your attorney will say, "He/she is responsible for this but not that." You can object to the prosecution's interpretation of the guidelines and the assignment of points. You can object to some of the other enhancements that add points. Even if your client knows he will be sentenced because he pleads guilty or is found guilty at trial, a person can still object at sentencing to try to reduce the number of points to reach a lower range of recommended imprisonment time. That is something else you would not have to deal with in the state court.

There really are significant differences between federal cases and state cases. They are different in scale, and the process is very different: from the method of investigation to the way in which sentences are given. Of course, the best way to approach any possible charge in either system is to avoid doing the crime in the first place, but people make mistakes. When they do, it is critically important that they find a capable attorney to get them through the system in the best way possible. You need to retain that attorney as early as possible in order to represent your interests early in the process. When you come against the resources of the federal government, you need all the help you can get.

(This content should be used for informational purposes only. It does not create an attorney-client relationship with any reader and should not be construed as legal advice. If you need legal advice, please contact an attorney in your community who can assess the specifics of your situation.)

40671401R00135